The ZX Spectrum on Your PC
Emulators, utilities and more

The ZX Spectrum on Your PC
Emulators, utilities and more

Second Edition

Colin Woodcock

Copyright © Colin Woodcock 2012
ISBN 978-1-4716-7621-5

All rights reserved

This paperback edition published in 2012

Colin Woodcock is hereby identified as author of this work in accordance with Section 77 of the Copyright, Designs and Patents Act 1988

Published by www.lulu.com

Cover design by Colin Woodcock.

All photography is copyright © Colin Woodcock 2012, except Figure 3.3 by JBattersby. This image obtained from *http://en.wikipedia.org/wiki/ZX_Printer* View photographs used for this book at *www.flickr.com/photos/79238217@N06/*

For Jack

Contents

Acknowledgements		*xi*
Preface to the Second Edition		*xiii*
Preface to the First Edition		*xv*
1	Emulator basics	1
	Spectrum models	2
	Virtual cassettes on your emulated Spectrum	5
	Snapshot files	11
	Disk/cartridge images	13
	ROM cartidges	20
	The keyboard	21
2	Finding files	24
3	Peripherals	29
	Joysticks	29
	Printers	31
	Other peripherals	35
	The MGT Plus D interface	37
	Television display	41
4	Emulator extras	44
	Input recording	44
	Audio/Video	46
	Graphics	47
	Other features	48

5	Utilities	49
	Graphics	50
	Programming	52
	Sound	58
	Organising your games/research	59
	Tape utilities	63
	'Depth' – a worked example	65
6	Spectrum clones	77
7	Other PC emulators	83
	EightyOne	84
	EmuZWin	85
	Es.pectrum	86
	Fuse	87
	RealSpectrum	88
	Speccy	89
	SpecEmu	90
	Spud	91
	UnrealSpeccy	91
	vbSpec	91
	Warajevo	91
	X128	92
	Zero	92
	ZX32	93
	Z80	93
8	Emulating homebrew hardware	94
	Storage	94
	Display	97
	Online connectivity	101

9	The ZX Spectrum on your portable device	103
	Spectaculator	105
	ZX Spectrum: Elite Collection	107
	Marvin	108
	Speccy	109
	ZXdroid	110
	ZXDS	110
Photography: The Art of Spectrum		115
Appendix A: About the ZX Spectrum		127
Appendix B: Some modern Spectrum games		143
Appendix C: 'Depth' program listing		169
Index		179

Acknowledgements

My thanks to Paul Dunn, Nick Humphries and Jonathan Needle, who proof-read the first edition of this book and made some very valuable suggestions (thanks again to Jon for jogging my memory on some Plus D stuff this time around). I also continue to be grateful to Matthew Westcott for helping me to get my head around TR-DOS.

Thanks also to Andrew Owen, who looked through the section in this second edition on ULAplus (and pointed me in that direction in the first place); his clear feedback was extremely helpful and timely.

I don't think I've ever thanked Shaun Bebbington properly for asking me to write the Spectrum entries for Micro Mart's 'Greatest ever home computer' competition. This led the way to a series of lengthier MM articles and then being asked by Martyn Carroll to write for the *Your Sinclair 94* project – arguably, my proudest Spectrum moment. Thank you Shaun.

And no Spectrum project of any sort would be complete without a big thank you to Martijn van der Heide at WoS (which has hosted the first edition of this book for eight years now); his contribution to the Spectrum scene continues to goes way beyond the easily measurable.

Preface to the Second Edition

I wrote The ZX Spectrum on Your PC during a brief spring holiday in Cornwall in 2004. Eight years have passed since then and the Sinclair ZX Spectrum is now thirty years old. Which is incredible. My teenage days spent on the Spectrum seem somehow a great deal more recent than, say, learning Word Perfect on a DOS PC or encountering Windows for the first time.

I left the Spectrum scene a good few years ago, having spent five years totally immersed in it. It was a wonderful, immensely productive period for me that re-ignited my passion for writing. In addition to the eleven editions of ZXF that I edited, I also wrote a number of articles for Micro Mart and for the special edition of Your Sinclair bundled with Retro Gamer issue 9.

And, of course, I wrote *The ZX Spectrum on Your PC*, which has been downloaded now many thousands of times and is often the direction signposted by regulars for newcomers to the World of Spectrum asking, "How do I get Spectrum games to work on my PC?" I am immensely proud of that and it gives me great pleasure to think that my book has been the way through which so many people have been able to revisit their childhood and teenage memories.

I left because it was time to move on to other things. But how could I ignore the thirtieth anniversary of the computer that gave me an advantage in life in so many ways? Eight years is also a long time for a nonfiction book to go without revision.

This edition is two things. Firstly, it's an update to my original book. A lot of the original text is still valid and has remained, however the Spectrum scene has moved on in the past few years and there are new things to report on. It's a much longer book than the original: more emulators are covered and there are also two new chapters – one covering the emulation of some of the modern 'homebrew' hardware and one about emulators on mobile devices.

Secondly, this edition is a personal celebration of my own Spectrum writing and creativity, and I've indulged myself in including a couple of appendices that gather together some of my articles for ZXF, Micro Mart and YS 94. I've also added new illustrations and photographs. Photography is another interest of mine and getting out my hardware collection to photograph it was a lot of fun; I hope Spectrum enthusiasts enjoy the images that resulted.

I hope everyone gets something from this book, even if it's just to whet your appetite for at least a few goes at one of your favourite games of your youth. Times have moved on and technology continues to amaze and liberate us, but it's still good to spend a few moments every now and then back in the days when it was all brand new and the future was undiscovered. And when everything fit into 48K.

CW, April 2012

Preface to the first edition

So you've finally realised. You think that new technology is great - of course you do - but ever since you packed away that old Spectrum in a box and taped up the lid something has most definitely been missing. At last you understand you were turning your back on more than just an obsolete computer. The good news is that you don't have to fish the box out from under the bed just yet (or lament its sale on ebay or at the local car boot): the Spectrum is one of the most emulated computers (if not *the* most emulated computer) on the planet and the quality of its emulation is just superb. Just about anything you used to do on your old Spectrum can now be done on a PC Spectrum emulator - *including* plugging in a cassette recorder to load your favourite games.

But where do you start? A search for "ZX Spectrum" on Google reveals over four million links, many of which - to even the most enthusiastic of returners - can appear to make absolutely no sense whatsoever. TZX? *RZX*? Snapshot? Chuntey? What's it all about?

Things have moved on since the days of "Start tape, then press any key." In this book I hope to make these developments a little easier to digest. We'll start by assuming you to be completely new to the modern Spectrum scene and deal with the basics of emulation, then build things up from there. Although the book is written with complete beginners in mind I hope also that it will be useful to a variety of Spectrum hobbyists at various stages of their ZX rehabilitation; if, like me, you've at some point spent time lurking in the shadows of the *World of Spectrum* website, wondering whether your one little question will be screamed at for its ignorance/naivety/ten thousand references in the FAQ, then I hope you'll find some answers here.

Have fun! That's what it's all about.

Chapter One
Emulator basics

The aim of this chapter is to get you using an emulator to load and play games - just the way you used to on the real thing. Where do we start? There is an enormous number of emulators to choose from, which you can do at *www.worldofspectrum.org/emulators.html* (currently I count nearly 200 different emulators there across more than 30 different platforms).

The first ever PC Spectrum emulator I used was the DOS version of Z80 by Gerton Lunter. I got hold of this around about 1994 (it came on a floppy disk) and installed it on my 286 PC. The emulator came with one or two games, but if you wanted more than that (of course, this was before the days of being able to download games in an instant from the internet) you had to build an interface so that you could plug a cassette player into your PC's parallel printer port. Soldering competently is not a skill I can claim to possess; it took me a long time and a lot of help to build that interface, only to then find when it was finished that loading games from a tape into a PC is just as unreliable as loading them into a real Spectrum was.

During the noughties, Spectrum emulators went from basic to cram-packed with features in a very short space of time. 2002 to mid 2003 in particular was a fantastic period of both competition and collaboration between a number of the top authors, during which standards were driven upwards a great deal in a very short space of time. Since I first wrote this introduction to Spectrum emulation in the summer of 2002 (as the first of a series of articles for ZXF magazine) there have been staggering improvements in many of the leading emulators. *Spectaculator*, for example, had only just added in support for the Spectrum 128 and +2 back then (versions 1 and 2 only emulated 48K Spectrums); *now* it supports the Spectrum +3 and +2A, the Russian *Pentagon* and *Scorpion* clones, emulation of ZX Microdrives, the ZX Printer, *and* it can accept input from a cassette recorder plugged in to your PC's line-in socket in one direction and squirt out loading tones through the speaker socket to your genuine-article Spectrum in the other. And there's plenty more besides that as well.

One consequence of this rate of change is that any attempt here to describe in too much detail the current state-of-the-art in emulation across the differing features of the very many emulators available will make the main body of the book excessively complicated and confusing to follow. To make things simple, therefore, I'll concentrate on just two emulators for the most part: the aforementioned *Spectaculator* by Jonathan Needle and *ZX SPIN* by the ZX SPIN Team (for reasons I'm not entirely clear about, some members of this team have expressed a desire to remain anonymous, but I don't think I'm breaking any injunctions by naming Paul Dunn as one of the key authors). Both emulators are packed with features, are easy to use and run on all Windows versions up to Windows 7. One important difference between them, however, is that *Spectaculator* – in my opinion, the eversoslightly more user-friendly of the two (although it's a tinnier difference now than it was when I wrote the first edition of this book) – is shareware (a 30 day free trial can be downloaded from www.spectaculator.com; after that you'll have to pay £20 to continue to use it, but you do then receive all subsequent updates for free) whilst *ZX SPIN* is free. Both emulators can be obtained from the emulators page at the *World of Spectrum* website (*www.worldofspectrum.org/emulators.html*).

But I won't be ignoring other emulators completely. In Chapter Seven, I'll present a selection of other emulators and their features. Along the way, some of these will also get a mention where we look at emulator features not covered by *Spectaculator* or *ZX SPIN*.

Spectrum models (just in case you'd forgotten)

The original ZX Spectrum, with its quirky rubber keys, was released by *Sinclair Research Ltd* in 1982. This model initially came in two versions - one with 16K RAM and one with 48K RAM. The 16K and 48K Spectrums both display the famous "© 1982 Sinclair Research Ltd" message when switched on and both employ the single keystroke method of entering keywords in BASIC (for example, the letter J would display LOAD when pressed at the flashing K prompt).

Fig 1.1 The original 16/48K rubber-keyed ZX Spectrum.

The *Spectrum+*, which came out in 1984 was essentially the 48K machine with a slightly better keyboard and a redesigned case. The Spectrum and Spectrum+ are therefore identical as far as emulation is concerned and most emulators make no distinction between them - they're just referred to as 48K on the list of models to emulate.

Fig 1.2 The ZX Spectrum+. A keyboard upgrade.

Shortly before its sale to *Amstrad Plc* in 1986, Sinclair released the *Spectrum+ 128*. Visually very similar to the Spectrum+ (Sinclair by this stage didn't have the money to develop a new case) this 128K RAM computer was distinguishable from its immediate predecessor by a black metal heat sink down the right hand side (now often affectionately referred to as the 'toast rack') which dissipated the extra heat generated by all the new memory chips. In addition to the extra memory, a 3 channel music chip was added too. A simple menu system was introduced and the single keystroke system was abandoned in favour of a letter-by-letter approach (so you had to type out the whole word).

Fig 1.3 The ZX Spectrum+ 128K, complete with 'toast rack' heatsink.

The *Spectrum +2* was Amstrad's first 128K Spectrum and also released in 1986. A grey machine with a proper keyboard (Alan Sugar is alleged to have said that the original rubber-keyed Spectrum looked like a "pregnant calculator"), this was the first Spectrum to incorporate a built-in tape deck. It was followed up in 1987 by the *Spectrum +3* - a return to black, with a 3 inch disk drive built in – and the *Spectrum +2A*, a black version of the +2 (which was essentially internally the same as the +3 but with a cassette deck).

In fact, there were many other versions of the Spectrum released in other countries – some official and others not – many of which can also be emulated by *Spectaculator, ZX SPIN* and other emulators. We'll take a closer look at these in a later chapter.

Emulator basics 5

Fig 1.4 The Amstrad Sinclair Spectrum +2A, slightly modified with the grey keys from the original +2 to give it a more 'Spectrumy look'. Yes.

Fig 1.5 The Amstrad Sinclair ZX Spectrum +3.

Virtual cassettes on your emulated Spectrum

Time to explain a bit about file formats. The Spectrum, of course, used cassette tape primarily as its storage medium. That's not to say that there weren't any other ways of saving and loading programs back then: the *Spectrum +3* had a built-in 3 inch disk drive, for example, and the original 48K Spectrum had a special *Microdrive* system developed for it by Sinclair Research. More on these later. There were also various add-on disk drive interfaces over the years that plugged in to the expansion connector on the back and allowed you to use standard 5.25 and 3.5 inch disk drives such as the *MGT Plus D* interface and the *Technology Research Ltd BETA* interface, and we'll look at these later on too. Despite these valiant attempts at bringing 'mass storage' to the Spectrum, however, cassette tape remained the firm favourite amongst Spectrum users, and this was the format that the vast majority of software for the machine was released on, right up to the last few commercial releases in 1993.

So most of your Spectrum memories are probably about games that you loaded from cassette: red, yellow and blue stripes, loading tones (some Spectrum users claim they can hear these even with the volume turned down) and - if you were unlucky - an 'R tape loading error' message. Any emulation of the 'Spectrum experience' just wouldn't be even complete without including all of this palava.

Now here's the deal with cassettes: a Spectrum program stored on tape rarely consisted of a *single file*. Your typical Spectrum game, for example, would usually consist of *at least* three files: the BASIC loader, followed by the loading screen usually and followed next by the main program code. Let's look briefly at each of these in turn.

The BASIC loader

The purpose of this small program is to prepare the Spectrum for the files to follow. When you type LOAD "" (or select Tape Loader from a 128 menu) the Spectrum expects a BASIC program; most games, however, are written in machine code and machine code has to be loaded with a different set of commands altogether (*LOAD "filename" CODE start address, file length*, for example, or *LOAD "filename" CODE* followed by *PRINT USR start address*). The BASIC loader, therefore, is a BASIC program that loads in and executes the remaining files for you (effectively entering these more complex commands on your behalf and saving you the hassle) - first the loading screen and then the main program code. The arrival of the BASIC loader would be announced by "Program: hobbit" (or whatever your game was called) in the top-left corner of the screen.

The loading screen

The loading screen was a code file loaded to the Spectrum's screen memory at machine code address 16384. If you didn't black out the screen first it would appear in a rather odd, line-by-line fashion.

The program code

The example in Figure 1.6 below is the BASIC loader listing for The Hobbit (this is about as simple as tape files come; as games got larger and more complicated, the number of program files on a cassette grew rapidly and it's actually quite rare for cassettes to have as few as three files in total). Here we see that line 5 clears out the memory to make way for what's coming, lines 10 and 20 black out the screen and prevent naughty hackers from BREAKing into the program, line 30 loads the loading screen into the screen memory and line 50 loads the main program code. Line 60 runs the main code (from address 27648) once it's loaded.

```
   5 CLEAR 24575
  10 BORDER 0: PAPER 0: INK 0: CLS
  20 POKE 23659,0: PRINT AT 22,0;;
  30 LOAD "p"CODE 16384
  40 POKE 23659,0: PRINT AT 22,0;;
  50 LOAD "h"CODE
  60 PRINT USR 27648
```

Fig 1.6 The Hobbit's BASIC loader

So it's not just a question of loading individual files into your virtual Spectrum; the *whole tape* that contains the files has to be simulated if Spectrum emulators are to remain faithful to the original experience. This is where the file formats *.TZX* and *.TAP* come in (the former being a more recent formulation and more authentic than the latter). A TZX file is, effectively, a *virtual cassette* that contains all the individual files necessary for the game to run, and your emulated Spectrum accesses this in just the same way as your original Spectrum did, loading the BASIC loader first and so on. Most emulators now come with a 'virtual cassette player,' that allows you to play, stop and forward/rewind the virtual cassette; *Spectaculator* even includes a record button and the option to insert a 'blank tape' for your own programs to be recorded on.

This book is primarily intended for people wanting to emulate their old Spectrum experiences on their Windows PC, but - as an aside - if you ever do decide to actually open that taped up old box in the attic and get out your *real* Spectrum to have a play on, you'll find yet another treat in store for you, courtesy of virtual cassette files and the featured Spectrum emulators. Using the 'boost loading tones' option in either *Spectaculator* (*Tools* menu > *Options* > *Cassette Recorder* > *'Boost loading noise volume'*) or ZX SPIN (*Tools* menu > *Options* > *Files* > *'Boost loading tones when playing'*) and running a lead from your PC's speaker out socket to your Spectrum's ear socket will enable you to load games from 'virtual' cassettes on your PC into your Spectrum, just as though they were real cassettes - the Spectrum can't tell the difference. Which means that most of the several thousand Spectrum titles to be found on the internet (more on this in Chapter Two) can be used directly on your real Spectrum as well as your emulator. How cool is that?

Loading from virtual cassette on Spectaculator

The simple way to do this is just to go to *File* menu, select *Open* and then navigate to the cassette file you're after. This will then automatically load the tape (and will do so instantly if you have flashload on or at normal tape loading speed if not). If you'd like to load a game the old fashioned way, however, follow the steps below.

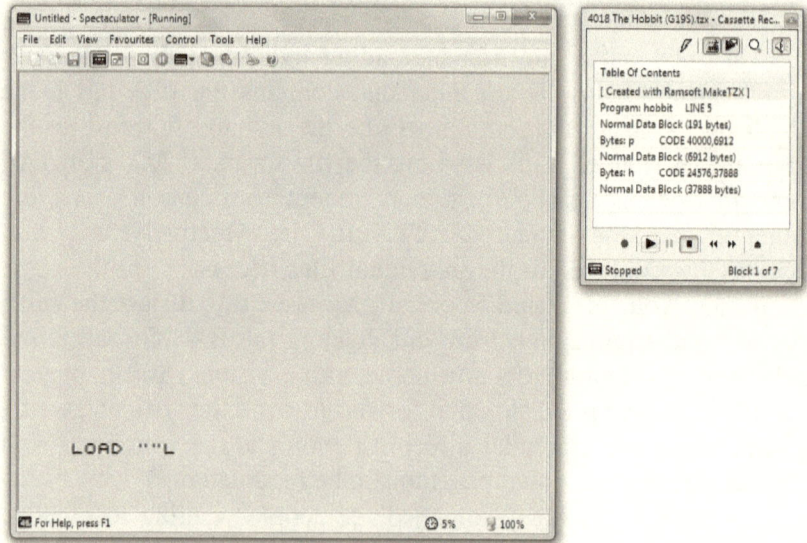

Fig. 1.7 Loading a tape file in Spectaculator.

1. Open the cassette recorder window: *View* > *Cassette Recorder*.

2. Select a cassette file to load into your virtual cassette recorder: *File > Open* (a cassette file will end in either .TAP or .TZX).

3. 48K users: on your emulated Spectrum type LOAD "" (LOAD can be found on the J key and the " symbol is obtained with a right shift and P) as shown in Fig. 1.7 above and hit ENTER.

4. 128K users: on your emulated Spectrum, select Tape Loader from the main menu and hit ENTER.

5. Click play on the tape recorder. Depending on whether you've selected flashloading or not (the little lightning symbol), the game will either instantly appear or load in 'real time,' loading tones, stripes and all.

Saving to virtual cassette on Spectaculator

1. To create a new, blank tape and insert it into the cassette recorder, all you have to do is select *File > New > Audio cassette file* and give your new tape file a name. In it goes.

2. Alternatively, you could choose an existing tape file and add your saves to the end of it. Find the tape and load it into the virtual cassette recorder with *File > Open* (again, remembering that a cassette file will end in either .TAP or .TZX).

3. In the main emulation window, type SAVE "filename" (SAVE resides on the S key if you're in 48K mode) and press ENTER.

4. Up comes the message, "Start tape, then press any key." Press record on the cassette recorder (the little red circle) then *click on the main emulator window* and press any key. Done.

Loading from virtual cassette on ZX SPIN

As with *Spectaculator,* the easiest way of doing this is just to go to *File* menu, select *Load file* and navigate to the tape file you're after. Your game will then load instantly. For those who like to do it properly, however, follow the steps below.

1. Open the cassette recorder window: *Tools > Tape Browser*. On the tape browser itself, go to the *Acceleration* menu and select *Normal Speed*.

2. The first time you use *ZX SPIN,* you'll need to turn off autoloading (unless, of course, you want tapes to load automatically). To do this, go to *Tools* menu and select *Options*. Select *Files* from the left side buttons and then *Tapes* from the horizontal tabs. Unclick the 'Load tapes automatically' and 'Start/Stop the tape automatically' boxes.

3. Select a cassette file to load into your virtual cassette recorder: *File > Load file* then navigate to your tape file in the usual way.

4. 48K users: on your emulated Spectrum type LOAD "" (LOAD can be found on the J key and the " symbol is obtained in *ZX SPIN* using *ctrl* and P) and hit ENTER.

5. 128K users: on your emulated Spectrum, select Tape Loader from the main menu and hit ENTER.

6. Click play on the tape recorder. The game will load. Incidentally, for those who want the *ultra* real loading experience, *ZX SPIN* can also generate tape hiss/wobble, making your loading tones sound just as crappy as those tape-to-tape C90 recordings (which, of course, you never even thought about making). Also just like those recordings, however, this option will increase the likelihood of getting an 'R Tape loading error' message or perhaps one of those messy loading screens with bits flashing that shouldn't be. Ah, the good old days. Kids these days don't know that they're born. And so on. To enable this wonderful option, go to *Tools* menu and select *Options*; select *Files* from the left side buttons and then *Tapes* from the horizontal tabs; tick the 'Simulate old tape player (Hiss/wobble)' box.

Saving to virtual cassette on ZX SPIN

To create a blank tape in *ZX SPIN*, select *Recording > Tape Recording > Insert Tape For Saving* and give your tape file a name (alternatively, if you want to save onto a tape file you created earlier, navigate to and select that instead). *ZX SPIN* is a little confusing in that this new tape doesn't now appear in your on-screen tape browser (it's a bit like having a second (invisible) tape recorder, just for saving on). But everything else is the same: type SAVE "filename" and hit ENTER, then hit any key at the "Start tape, then press any key" message. Later, when you want to load back from your tape, follow the steps above for '*Loading from virtual cassette on ZX SPIN*'.

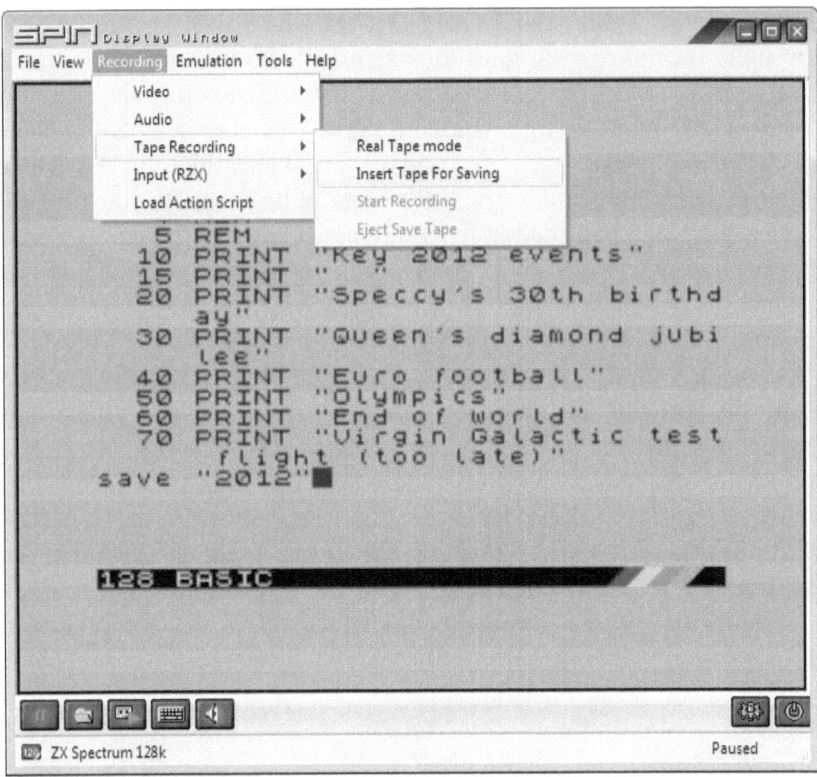

Fig. 1.8 Saving in ZX SPIN.

Snapshot files

Before virtual cassette files (or 'Cassette images,' as they're sometimes called) were sorted out, the mainstay of the spectrum emulator was the 'snapshot file'. A snapshot file is essentially a memory dump (or 'snapshot') of the Spectrum's memory at any given point - most game snapshot files that you can download from the Internet have been saved (or 'snapped') just at the point at which they've loaded. The origins of this file format go back to the days of the original Spectrum hardware: with all these add on disk drive devices (and eventually the +3 three inch drive) a way had to be thought of for transferring existing software owned by an individual from tape to disk (where was the point in owning a posh new disk drive if you couldn't use it to speed up the loading of all your favourite games?) Most games protected their BASIC loader from easy hacking, hiding the listing (and therefore the start addresses) through special tricks that left a blank screen and perhaps a copyright message, so it wasn't just a matter of loading the file into memory and then saving it back onto disk with a new BASIC loader modified as appropriate. Disk drive interfaces such as the MGT Plus D, therefore, sported a little snap button which you pressed once your game had loaded from tape; at this point the game would freeze and you were able to save it - as it was, at that precise moment - to disk.

So a snapshot file - in contrast to a virtual cassette file - really is just *one file*. You don't get the BASIC loader or the loading screen with this sort of file; when you load it back in you just go straight back to the point at which you saved the file, be that at the start of a game or somewhere in the middle (at the end of a level, for example, so you don't have to play the game right from the beginning next time). Snapshot files were great at the time - a convenient way of loading a favourite game quickly - but as emulators developed and the pangs of nostalgia for the good old days grew, something more authentic was required; also snapshots were no good for multi-load games (where each level in a game had to be loaded separately from tape). These days, therefore, the preferred format for distributing Spectrum software in is cassette format; snapshot files are mainly used for saving your progress in a game.

The two main snapshot formats - both of which have been around for years - are *.SNA* and *.Z80*; both are supported by the vast majority of emulators (and both support also 48k and 128k snapshots). More recently, Jonathan Needle developed a new snapshot format called .SZX for *Spectaculator*. SZX files include *hardware state* information and this is a reflection of sorts of just how far emulation has come since the formulation of .SNA and .Z80. An SZX file, therefore, doesn't just save the state of your Spectrum at the point of snapping, but also the state of any peripherals - most importantly the cassette recorder and any disk drives. So say, for example, that you load up a multiload game from cassette into an emulated Spectrum +2 and make it to the end of level two of the game before SZX snapshotting it; the next time you load that SZX file into *Spectaculator* the emulator will switch to +2 mode, load in your game at the point at which it was snapped and insert the relevant cassette into the cassette recorder (in the position it was in when the save took place).

Both *Spectaculator* and *ZX SPIN* support .SNA, .Z80 and .SZX files. To load these, simply go to *File* menu and on *Spectaculator* select *Open* and on *ZX SPIN* select *Load file*. Then navigate to your file and select it.

Disk/cartridge images

And so to 'mass media'. There were two 'official' mass media formats for the Spectrum: Sinclair's own *Microdrive* system for the Spectrum, Spectrum+ and Spectrum 128 (microdrives - of which you could attach eight - plugged into the Sinclair *Interface 1*); and the 3 inch disk drive built into the Spectrum +3. Both systems are supported by both *Spectaculator* and *ZX SPIN*.

In the same way that cassette file formats such as .TAP and .TZX work as 'virtual cassettes,' so disk file formats work as 'virtual disks' or 'disk images'. Pop the image file into its drive via the appropriate emulator tool and then access it from within your emulated Spectrum in exactly the way you would have done on the real thing. For +3 disk images the standard file format is .DSK and for microdrive cartridge images the standard file format is .MDR.

Working with Microdrives

In the year following the Spectrum's launch, Sinclair Research released the Interface 1 and Microdrive expansion system; the former an interface styled in the same curves of the Spectrum that screwed into the base of the machine, the latter a looped tape system not entirely dissimilar to the old eight track music cartridges. The added functionality of these devices was 'phase two' of the Spectrum's planned development, giving life to the previously redundant drive commands (CAT, FORMAT and so on) printed below the Spectrum's number keys.

Fig 1.9 The Microdrive plugged into the Interface 1, which sat beneath the Spectrum. Up to eight in a row could be connected.

Microdrive cartridges were tiny: 30x42x5mm; they contained 15m of 1.9mm tape driven by a rather noisy little motor at the breakneck speed of about two metres per second. They could typically store between 90 and 100KB of data, of which 6K could be loaded in close to four seconds. And up to eight drives could be connected at once via the IF1, giving a total online storage capacity of nearly 800KB. These were Sinclair's on-the-cheap answer to the much more expensive floppy disk systems of the day, although compared to disk systems they were inferior in many ways and it's probably more appropriate to think of them as an advanced tape system.

Fig 1.10 Microdrive cartridges contained a 15m spool of tape that whizzed around at two metres per second.

Microdrives were notoriously unreliable. Tape that thin moving at that speed was unlikely to last forever - even the manual cautioned against expecting this - but also early cartridge design placed the rough bits from the moulding process on the inside of the cartridge case to make it look better, giving the high speed tape something pointy to catch and snag on. Not good. Nonetheless, Sinclair staked a lot on the Microdrive system, using a slightly modified version for his QL computer also. The format received extremely limited support from software developers, however, and after the sale of Sinclair computers to Amstrad it was effectively killed off.

The microdrive was one of three expansion possibilities to the Spectrum offered by the ZX Interface 1, the other two being the local area network (you could connect up to 64 Spectrums) and the RS232 serial port. Sinclair wanted to keep the basic syntax for all three of these the same and the result was not for the faint hearted. When entering a LOAD/SAVE/FORMAT, etc command you not only had to identify the destination of the data (ie, microdrive, network or RS232), but the number of the drive or station too. So:

LOAD*"m";2;"Squares"   would load the program "Squares" from microdrive 2 but;

LOAD*"n";5   would load a program from network station 5 and;

SAVE*"b"   would send your program to the RS232 port ('b' is for binary as opposed to 't' for text).

Not only does *Spectaculator* offer support for microdrives (you can have up to 8, just like the real thing) and the IF1's RS232, it also emulates the microdrive's motor sound!

1. To enable the ZX Interface 1, select *Tools > Options > Hardware*. Make sure your hardware is either 48K ZX Spectrum or Spectrum 128 and tick the *ZX Interface 1 and Microdrives* box.

2. *View > Microdrives* brings up the microdrive panel, from which you can load .MDR cartridge files (click on the word 'Empty' beside the drive number). You can also load a microdrive cartridge from *Spectaculator's* main *File* menu by selecting *Open* (the same way you would for a tape or snapshot file) and navigating from there to your .MDR file. Once selected, the cartridge will appear in the Microdrive window.

3. To add additional microdrives, select *Tools > Options > ZX Interface 1*.

4. To insert a blank cartridge, choose *File > New > Microdrive cartridge*.

And here's how to work with microdrives in *ZX SPIN:*

1. To enable the ZX Interface 1, select *Tools > Options >*

Hardware. Make sure your hardware is one of the Sinclair models (16K, 48K, 48K+ or 128K) then click on the *Peripherals* tab. Tick the *Sinclair Interface 1* box.

2. *File > Microdrives* brings up the microdrive panel. You should be able to see the words 'No Cartridge Inserted' in grey and repeated several times. There are actually eight of these – one for each Microdrive – and clicking on one will highlight it and add a button with '...' to the right. Clicking on the button will enable you to navigate to a .MDR file.

3. To insert a blank cartridge, click on the Create New button at the bottom of the Microdrives window and give your new cartridge file a name.

Working with +3 disks

In 1987 Amstrad released the first and only Spectrum to feature a built-in disk drive - the Spectrum +3. It used a 3 inch drive system capable of storing 180K per side (you had to take the disk out and turn it over). The choice of this format as opposed to the more popular (and larger capacity) 3½ inch disk (the little black/blue, plastic squares which became what most people thought of as 'floppy disks') had a lot to do with Amstrad's own stake in it – the company owned a large quantity of the drives and also manufactured the disks. Other computers manufactured by Amstrad (the PCW range of personal computers and the disk-based CPC home computers launched to compete against the Spectrum and the Commodore 64) also used this format.

Amstrad's +3 disk system was much simpler to use than microdrives were. Essentially you just used the same old commands you were used to using with tape:

LOAD "squares"
SAVE "squares" LINE 1
VERIFY "squares"

And so on. You could change back to tape by typing in SAVE "t:" before any save commands or LOAD "t:" before any loads (to switch to disk again type LOAD/SAVE "a:"

Fig 1.11 The 3 inch drive was located to the right of the keyboard. Disks had to be turned over in order to access all 360K storage capacity.

+3 disks are emulated using the .DSK file format. The standard disk used – as mentioned – was a 360K 3" CF2 disk (180K per side), but you could also plug into the +3 a standard 3.5" 720K disk drive via the computer's Drive B port. Both *Spectaculator* and *ZX SPIN* will allow you to create either disk image and to emulate the external drive B.

In *Spectaculator:*

1. Select the ZX Spectrum +3 via *Tools > Options > Hardware*.

2. With *Options* still open, click on the *Spectrum +3* tab and tick the 'Enable drive B' box if you would like to emulate both the internal and external drives.

3. *View > Disk Drives* brings up the disk drives panel, from which you can load .DSK disk files (click on the word 'Empty' beside the drive number). As with all other formats recognised by *Spectaculator,* you can also load a disk from *Spectaculator's* main *File* menu by selecting *Open* and navigating from there to the file you're after. Once selected, the disk will appear in the

disk drives panel.

4. To create and insert a blank disk, choose *File > New > Blank +3 Disk*. You will then be asked how you would like to format the disk (as a 3 inch or 3.5 inch disk) and which drive to insert it into (if you've enabled the external drive B).

In *ZX SPIN:*

1. Select the ZX Spectrum +3 via *Tools > Options > Hardware*.

2. *Tools > Disk options* brings up the disk drives panel, from which you can load .DSK disk files (click on the folder icon to locate your file) into either the internal or external drive. Unlike *Spectaculator's* disk drives panel, the *ZX SPIN* panel does not remain open alongside the main emulator window. Once you've selected your disk(s), click *Okay* to return to your emulated +3.

3. To create and insert a blank disk, click on *Create* New at the disk drives panel and select your desired format from the drop down list.

+3 software

Although the Spectrum +3's disk format never really took over as the main Spectrum storage media (it was – quite simply – too little too late), there were still quite a few great titles released on the format that are well worth exploring. These even included titles which were not made available on tape, such as some of the wonderful Magnetic Scrolls text adventures (for example, the beautifully written Jinxter, albeit without any of the sumptuous graphics that accompanied it on other computer formats) and Douglas Adams' Infocom masterpiece, *The Hitchhiker's Guide to the Galaxy*. You can browse over a thousand +3 disk images at a special WoS (see next chapter) section for the format. This can be found at *www.worldofspectrum.org/disks.html.*

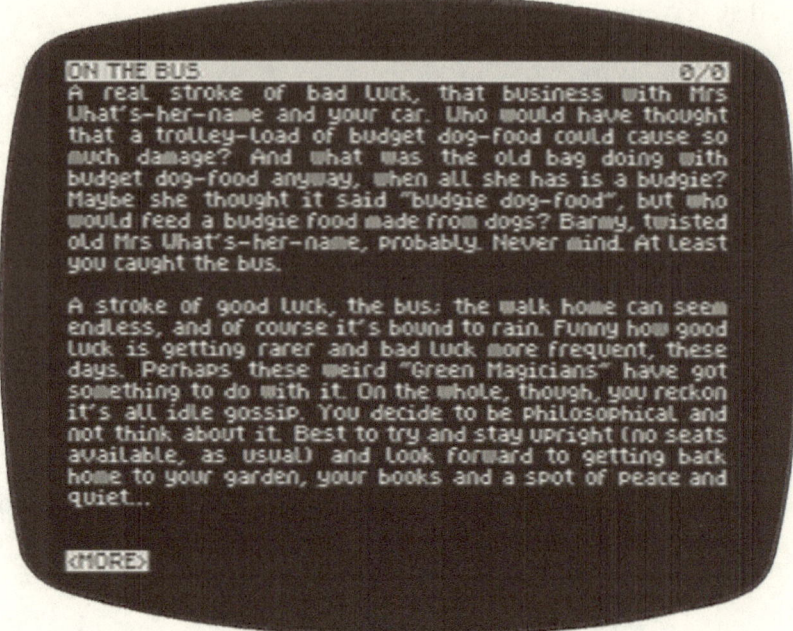

Fig 1.12 Jinxter (by Magnetic Scrolls) running on the Spectrum +3.

Other disk systems

As mentioned earlier, there were plenty of other add-on disk drive devices for the Spectrum in its time; we'll have a closer look at a couple of these later in the book.

ROM cartridges

It's perhaps worth mentioning ROM cartridges. Although the vast majority of Spectrum software was released on cassette, Sinclair did release an additional interface for the Spectrum – at around about the time of the Interface 1 – into which ROM cartridges could be inserted. These had an advantage over cassette software in that they loaded instantly, the moment you turned on your Spectrum. The *Interface 2* was released simultaneously with ten titles on ROM cartridge; these were all games which had already proven popular with Spectrum users rather than brand new software and the ROM cartridge versions were considerably more expensive than their cassette counterparts. They sold very badly. No software companies ever released games in this format and Sinclair itself released no additional titles.

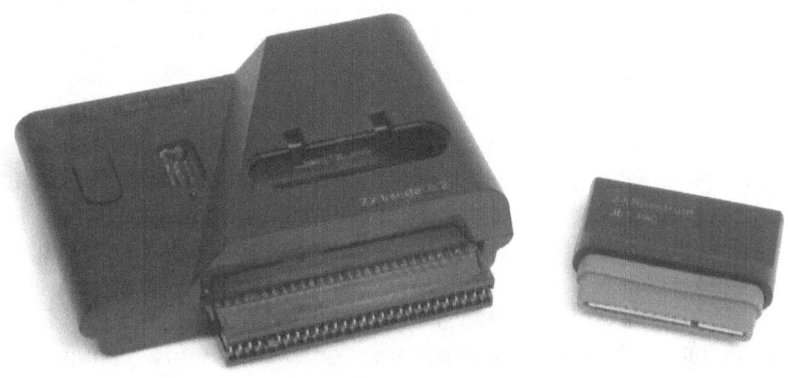

Fig 1.13 The ZX Interface 2 with a ROM cartridge. The interface also doubled as a joystick interface for the Sinclair joystick standard.

There are a few Spectrum emulators which support the ZX Interface 2, however this is mostly a 'for the sake of completeness' feature which doesn't actually add any functionality (since the original games can be loaded in an instant anyway using the flashload option).

The keyboard

By now you should pretty much know all you need in order to get back to playing those favourite games from your more youthful times - the next chapter will tell you where to get the games themselves from, and you might just decide at that point you need read no further. It's worth paying brief attention, however, to the business of the Spectrum keyboard before pushing on, even if it's just to remind yourself which key the quotation marks are on.

Of course, from the Spectrum 128 onwards there was no need to type anything into your Spectrum at all to load a game - just hit enter at the main menu to go into the 'Tape Loader' and then press play on your cassette deck. Regardless, just as we often seem to forget that not all Spectrums had rubber keys, still we mostly associate playing games in those days with having to type LOAD "" first! And let's be honest - no matter how much of a die-hard gamer you were or still are, it's nice to be able to dip back into ZX BASIC every now and again. The problem that emulation brings to this, however, is that our PC keyboards lack those essential keywords for the single keystroke method employed by the 48K model, plus all the symbols (for example, the quotation marks) are in the wrong places! How do we get around this? Well, there are a few ways.

One of the things that distinguishes *Spectaculator* from other emulators is its great help system. Pretty much a reference document in its own right, the help menu also includes a 'keyboard map' in which you can look up keywords and symbols (or 'tokens' as they are also known) to find out the keyboard combinations required to get to them. There's also a 'Virtual Keyboard' obtained via the Help menu. Selecting this brings up a separate window containing a photographic 48K rubber-keys keyboard that you can operate by clicking on the keys with your mouse. As a method of information entry, it's rather slow compared to actual typing; but for single keystroke BASIC programming (or even just typing in a LOAD command) it's a great timesaver compared to having to keep on working out what combination of keys on your laptop activate extended mode.

ZX SPIN also has a virtual keyboard, in fact *SPIN* was the emulator to first come up with the idea. The '48K Keyboard Helper', available from the *Tools* menu, has two other modes too – *Command Finder*, which allows you to select individual commands from a menu and send them straight to the Spectrum and *Quick BASIC*, which allows you to type whole lines of BASIC straight into a text box that can then be checked for errors and sent to the Spectrum at the click of a button. It's a massively helpful tool.

Another way around the 48K keyboard problem is to use a customised ROM that allows keywords to be entered on a letter-by-letter basis (just like the 128 did), rather than using the single keystroke approach (PRINT on P, LOAD on J, etc). The 48K Spectrum had a 16K ROM (Read Only Memory, essentially the operating system of the Spectrum) and a number of alternatives to it have been designed within the Spectrum community over the years. A couple of fine examples of these are the *Gosh Wonderful* ROM by *Geoff Wearmouth* and the *SE Basic* ROM by *Andrew Owen*, both of which allow you to type keywords letter-by-letter whilst maintaining compatibility with most existing Spectrum software. It makes the business of typing on an emulated 48K a great deal easier. You can download the *Gosh Wonderful* ROM from Philip Kendall's *Spectrum ROMs collection* web page at *www.srcf.ucam.org/~pak21/spectrum/roms.pl*. To install it in *Spectaculator*, select *Tools > Options > Advanced;* click on the (None) next to '16K/48K Spectrum' in the *Custom ROMs* section; locate the GW ROM and select it. In *SPIN*, select *Tools > Options > Hardware > ROM Images* and navigate to the ROM Image you are after by clicking on the folder icon. Andrew Owen's *SE BASIC* is actually built-in to *SPIN,* however, so you don't actually have to go to the trouble of finding and downloading this ROM: beneath the ROM Image selection box just described there is a 'with SE BASIC' box – tick this and click on Okay.

Fig 1.13 SE BASIC running in 48k Spectrum mode in ZX SPIN.

Chapter Two
Finding software

So where do we get these games and other files from? This part is *really* simple.

The Spectrum community is blessed by the work of a chap called *Martijn van der Heide;* his site - *World of Spectrum,* more commonly referred to as 'WoS' (*www.worldofspectrum.org*) - contains the biggest archive of Spectrum files on the planet - nearly 25,000 titles at present. There's not an emulation site that I know of - Spectrum or otherwise - that comes even remotely close to this sort of content - and it's all completely free.

WoS was started in November 1995 by Martijn, initially as a web page to host his Spectrum games database program, *SGD*. In January 1997 the site started hosting games downloads (opening with some three-and-a-half thousand titles) and it's been updated pretty much on a weekly basis ever since.

If you can't get hold of the title you're after amongst the thousands at WoS, it's probably either 'missing in action' (also known as 'MIA,' these missing files are listed at WoS and it's always worth checking any old tapes you have - or any you pick up at the local car boot sale - against this, just in case you've got something that's needed) or it's distribution has been denied by the original copyright owner. Martijn has been working tirelessly over the years to contact a huge number of game authors, publishers and intellectual property owners in order to establish whether or not they mind their work being distributed for free via WoS; a small number have told him that in fact they *do* mind (for example, *Ultimate* and *Codemasters*) and in these cases the relevant titles are immediately withdrawn from the site. WoS is one of the very few (if not the only) emulation sites on the web that goes about proactively seeking distribution permission in this way, and the approach has won it a lot of friends and a great deal of respect (authors approached hardly ever say no).

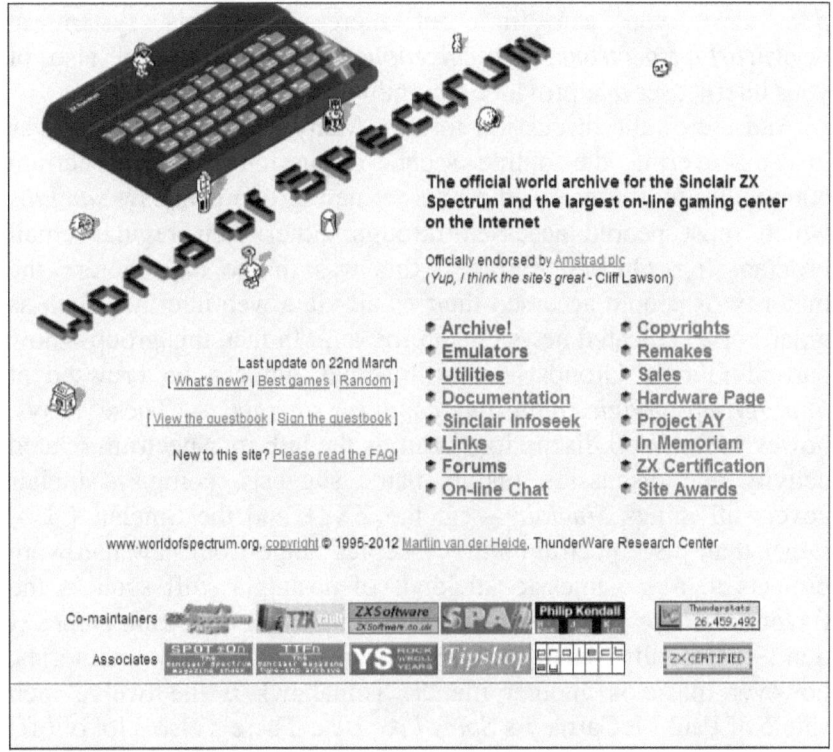

Fig 2.1 www.worldofspectrum.org is the largest online gaming centre in the world. Most of the 23,000 titles listed there can be played within your web browser via a Java emulator (ZZ Spectrum).

It's not just games you can download from WoS either. Aiming to bring you pretty much "anything and everything from the Spectrum era," the site also hosts inlay card scans, instructions for games, complete books, complete magazine scans and a whole host of modern software downloads: emulators, utilities and more. There's also an enormous range of documentation available, from the original Spectrum introduction booklet and other manuals to circuit diagrams, schematics and servicing information. PDFs of books at WoS tend to consist of page scans rather than formatted text (which would take considerably more time to create); similarly, magazines are arranged in folders of individual page scans. Download sizes can quickly mount up, therefore, so be mindful of the WoS daily download limit. Currently, this is set at 10,000 'credits' per day (complete books are 250 credits each, magazine full page scans are 2 credits per page and all other material is 1 credit per item); you can find out more about this system at *www.worldofspectrum.org/archivenote.html*. Be mindful also of your internet service provider's monthly download limit.

And there's the discussion forum. Many years ago, when I was just discovering the online scene, discussion in the Spectrum community took place in the internet newsgroup *comp.sys.sinclair*, which most people accessed through either their regular email program (eg, Outlook Express; this was in the days before the majority of people accessed their email via a web interface such as gmail) or a dedicated news client program. In fact, this group – now part of Google Groups – is still active and can be browsed at *http://groups.google.com/group/comp.sys.sinclair*. These days, however, the WoS discussion forum is the hub for Spectrum related activity and discussion (as its name suggests, comp.sys.sinclair covers all things *Sinclair* – eg, the ZX81 and the Sinclair QL – rather than just Spectrum stuff). Topics range from new hardware projects to new games to all kinds of nostalgia stuff such as the flavour of crisps you most associate with playing Spectrum games (I don't personally have any Spectrum-related food memories, however music is another matter: Tomahawk *is* the twelve inch single of Paul McCartney's *Spies Like Us*). There's also a lot of off-topic discussion there too (which, depending on your capacity for moans about what young people today/the country/the world is coming to when we live in a plentiful nation and millions elsewhere don't even have a toilet to take a shit in, you can take or leave at your leisure).

WoS will probably be the only site you'll ever need to visit for Spectrum files if you're just looking for old favourites to play again. After a while of playing around with these, however, you *might* just start feeling the need to explore some of the more recent software releases for the Spectrum. *People are still making new games for the Spectrum?* Oh yes.

An example is *www.cronosoft.co.uk*. A UK software label operating since early 2003, Cronosoft have been producing software for a number of 8 bit formats, including the Spectrum. Cronosoft titles can be bought on cassette, most titles selling for £3.99. I wholeheartedly recommend *Fun Park*, a 16K game developed by Jonathan Cauldwell from his original 4K entry in the 2003

Minigame coding competition.

There are plenty of other teams and individuals producing Spectrum software, many of whom do so for free and release their titles as .TZX files from either their own website or the World of Spectrum website (or both). The best way to find new releases at WoS is to click on the 'What's new' link on the front page of the site and scroll down the entries looking for items tagged 'Brand new software'. All of these titles are, of course, available from the main software database, however this is organised alphabetically so it's not immediately obvious which entries are the most recent.

Other places giving information about new Spectrum games are 'Retro Gamer,' a monthly publication from Imagine Publishing, and Shaun Bebbington's weekly 'Retro' column in Dennis Publishing's 'Micro Mart'. Both are available from newsagents. As a taster of releases since the year 2000, I've included in the appendices a selection of my own new game reviews from the period in which I was most active in the Spectrum scene (2002 to 2007). These include reviews from Micro Mart and the special edition Your Sinclair issue 94, as well as from my own publication ZXF.

Finally, no section on Spectrum software would be complete without a reference to the demo scene. You might recall from your Spectrum youth the odd game here and there that in some way broke the rules of what was and what wasn't considered possible for the Spectrum: more than one note being played at the same time on 48K titles, for example (many of the Codemasters games featured this), digitised speech (eg, *Ghostbusters*), graphics in the border (eg, the bicycle handlebars in *Paperboy*), more than two colours per 8x8 character (eg, the high score table in *Uridium*); the Spectrum isn't just remembered for its technical limitations, it's remembered also for the way in which many of those technical limitations were overcome in some way. Don't forget that the 48K Spectrum held a software market for over ten years; at today's pace of change – particularly where computers (rather than dedicated consoles) are concerned – that would be unthinkable. So finding new little tricks to wow players was an important part of game authoring back then, where today's developers hardly get a chance to fiddle with new technology before it's become obsolete. Have you ever found yourself wondering what could be achieved with today's technology if it was really pushed to its limits in the same way that the Spectrum's was?

As it happens, that's not an unanswered question. The PC demo scene attempts exactly that. Though it's now quite old, the '.the .product' demo by fr-08 (*www.theproduct.de*) still stagers me at what can be squeezed down into *under* 64K if everything is defined mathematically. If you've never seen this beautiful creation, consider yourself obliged to check it out (there's a video of it also at *www.youtube.com/watch?v=1dcrV_7JpXQ*).

Just as the PC demo scene pushes technology to its limits, then, so the Spectrum demo scene continues to push new things out of the Speccy. The vast majority of these programs are purely watch-only because achieving these effects and *at the same time* doing things like monitoring the keyboard/joystick for input and moving sprites about on the screen in response to this (as would be the requirement for a game) is just too much for the Spectrum to handle at the same time. When it comes to special graphics effects, timing is everything and the time required to scan the keyboard is time required to – effectively – manually switch the colour of the TV beam (this is how multicolour and border effects are achieved). Demo technology does sometimes make it into gameplay, however. Weird Science's 'TV Game,' for example, very effectively incorporates controllable border bats into its Pong-style game (see Appendix B for a review of this title).

But demos are still immense fun to watch and marvel at. To obtain the latest titles, you'll have to be prepared to do a little web searching, but many of the classics up to 2006 (my favourite is probably 'Binary Love') are available still from Matthew Westcott's *Demotopia* site at *www.zxdemo.org* and WoS has a small demos section to the archive also. You should also be aware that many of the best demos were coded in Eastern Europe, where a number of Spectrum clones were developed before the end of the cold war due to the unavailability of western technology; when running these titles, therefore, you will need to select the appropriate clone from *Spectaculator's* hardware menu. We'll cover Spectrum clones in more detail in a later chapter, so don't worry if that sounds confusing right now.

Chapter Three
Peripherals

So far we've looked at the two parts of the Spectrum experience you couldn't avoid, even if you only ever used the computer for games playing: using the keyboard and loading a program in from your storage device. Of course, if you *were* a die-hard games fan, it's likely there was a further piece of hardware you were used to interacting with on a regular basis - a joystick.

Fig 3.1 The Quickshot joystick.

There were lots of different joysticks made during the Spectrum's era; you plugged them into the Spectrum via joystick interfaces, each of which worked according to one of a small number of interface standards. The *Kempston* standard configured the interface as part of the Z80 Input/Output map, whilst the *Cursor* standard simply linked the joystick's movements to the cursor keys 5 to 8 (the keys with the little arrows on them) with 0 as fire; the *Sinclair* standard took the same approach as *Cursor*, using instead the keys 6 to 9 with 0 again as fire (the *Sinclair* standard supported two joysticks and keys 1 to 5 were used for joystick two). Selecting *Cursor* or *Sinclair* (the *Sinclair* standard was also sometimes referred to as *Interface 2,* since it was introduced through Sinclair's ZX Interface 2 – as discussed in Chapter One, an interface that plugged into the back of your Spectrum and allowed you to plug in two joysticks and a ROM cartridge) control for a game, therefore, would allow you to use the keyboard if you wanted (ie, keys 5 to 8 for *Cursor;* 6 to 9 for *Sinclair*); selecting *Kempston* would not.

Fig 3.2 The Quickshot connected to the Spectrum via the Kempston interface.

Having three different standards for joystick interfaces created a bit of a problem, since not all games produced gave you all three options on their control menus (and they generally didn't say on the box which standards they *did* support). If you used a *Cursor* interface, for example, and bought a copy of *Exolon* (which supports only *Kempston* and *Sinclair*), your joystick would be staying in its box whilst that game was on. The way around all of this was to shell out for one of the more expensive interfaces that had three joystick sockets on them - one for each standard.

The good news is you don't really have to worry about any of this with emulators, since all three standards are supported. All you need is a PC joystick or control pad plugged in to your usual game port; selecting which standard you want is simplicity itself: for *Spectaculator*, just select *Control > Joystick* and then the standard of your choice; for *ZX SPIN*, select *Tools > Options > Controllers* and the *Joystick* tab. Don't forget you'll have to select that standard from within the game itself also. *Kempston* is probably the best-supported standard generally, so selecting this in your emulator set-up will probably mean less fiddling in the future.

If you don't have a joystick, you can still map your PC keyboard's arrow keys onto one of the standards. For *Spectaculator*, select *Control > Keyboard Joystick* and then select the standard you intend to use ingame (Tab or right Alt acts as the fire button). For *SPIN*, select *Tools > Options > Controllers* and select the Keyboard tab (Control acts as fire). Then, from the *Emulation* menu, click on *Enable Keystick*.

Printers

After joystick interfaces, the next most common category of hardware to have been plugged into the Spectrum is probably printers. There were a number of ways of achieving this: for 48K Spectrums it had to be via an interface plugged into the machine's edge connector, of course; for the 128 and Amstrad's follow-up +2 a BT-style RS232 socket built-in could connect to standard serial printers of the day; and the +3 and +2A featured a Centronics port that could connect to standard parallel printers.

Sinclair actually had his own printing solution for the Spectrum on the market *before* the Spectrum came out. The *ZX Printer* was actually designed for the Spectrum's predecessor, the *ZX81*, but was just as happy hanging off the back of a Spectrum (happier, in fact, since the Spectrum could power the printer without the need for the separate power supply required by the ZX81).

But the *ZX Printer* was never intended as a way of printing out CVs, essays or your letters of complaint to the BBC; the little, silver 'toilet rolls' weren't exactly the most attractive presentation of text on paper and were seen as a cheap way of creating hard copies of program listings, nothing more. Printer resolution matched exactly the screen resolution, restricting you to the same 32 columns of text you got on the telly, all in the glorious Sinclair typeface. You could also do screendumps of whatever was on the Spectrum's screen (although, of course, all of the colour information would be lost). The *ZX Printer* worked by passing an electric current across the aluminium coating on the paper, effectively burning the surface to create the black 'ink.' It was a rather noisy process; a much quieter option was the *Alphacom 32* printer (known in the US as the *Timex Sinclair 2040*), a thermal printer that gave exactly the same output as the *ZX Printer*, but which used white paper that turned black (or blue, depending on the paper) when exposed to the heat.

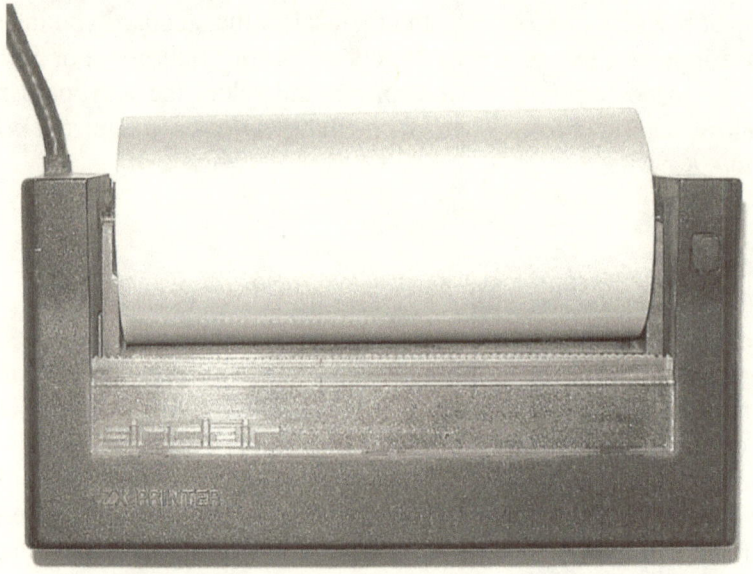

Fig 3.3 The ZX Printer was originally developed for the Sinclair ZX81 (image by Jbattersby).

So serious word processing programs for the Spectrum, such as *Tasword*, didn't really expect you to be printing your literary creation off on the *ZX Printer*. These, in fact, were assuming a much more standard printer to be attached via an interface or - for later software - via the RS232 or Centronics ports: a dot matrix printer, for example, of the sort ordinarily attached to an office computer. Spectrum emulators aren't able to emulate these specific printers in the way they are able to pretend to be a *ZX Printer*, of course, however a very powerful feature of *Spectaculator* is that it *can* intercept the printer output sent by the emulated Spectrum and redirect it to a text file which you can then load into a normal Windows word processor. Just think - all those teenage masterpieces you created might not be lost for good after all! How you set up their retrieval will depend on the model of Spectrum you are emulating plus the way the Spectrum software you want to print from is configured; have a look at the walk-through below for a guided example.

Working with the ZX Printer

Both ZX SPIN and Spectaculator support the ZX Printer. To enable it in *Spectaculator*, select *Tools > Options > Hardware* and tick the box for ZX Printer. You'll then need to open the printer output window (ie, so that you can actually see what's been printed): do this by going to the *View* menu and clicking on *ZX Printer*. *ZX SPIN* does not need to have the printer enabled (it automatically connects it when in 48K mode). To open the printer output window, select *Tools > ZX Printer Output*.

In Spectrum BASIC, the printer is accessed via the commands LPRINT and LLIST (the extra L stands for 'Line') and COPY. LPRINT will print text directly to the printer (so LPRINT "hello" would cause the word 'hello' to be printed), LLIST will send the current program listing to the printer and COPY will copy whatever's at that moment on the screen to the printer. Each time you send something to the printer, the Spectrum just sticks it straight underneath whatever was there before. *Spectaculator* does not support the little form feed button – *ZX SPIN* does (the little up arrow button in the printer output window) – so if you need to insert some space, send blank lines (ie, LPRINT "").

To copy protected loading screens, try using the *Multiface 1* interface (*Tools > Options > Multiface* to enable it in *Spectaculator*, then Ctrl-M to activate it). Pressing 'c' on the Multiface menu will send whatever image is on the screen straight to the printer. Don't forget, the printer interprets any INK colour as black and any PAPER colour as white, so what you see on the screen isn't always what you get on paper.

Converting a Tasword file with Spectaculator

Let's suppose you have some old Tasword files on cassette you want to convert to a standard text file for editing in your favourite Windows word processor. The first thing we need to do is configure *Spectaculator* so that it redirects printer output to a named text file. We'll be using a 128K version of Tasword to do the printing since the 48K version only supports the *ZX Printer* or other printers via a plug-in interface (not supported by *Spectaculator*); Tasword 128, however, sends its output by default to the RS232 port (which *is* supported). You can get hold of Tasword 128, of course, from *www.worldofspectrum.org* - look for it in the *Utilities* section of the Archive.

1. Before you load Tasword 128, go to the main Options box (*Tools > Options*) and select *Communications Ports*. In the *RS232 Serial Port* section select 'File' for *Send to* and then enter a filename in the text box beside this. I've chosen 'RS232.txt' and, for simplicity's sake, saved it in the root directory on C drive.

2. Now load up Tasword 128 in the usual way: insert the tape image into the virtual cassette recorder, select Tape Loader from the 128's main menu and press play. When Tasword has loaded, eject the cassette.

3. Now that Tasword has loaded, we need to tell *Spectaculator* to expect its next input from a real, rather than virtual cassette. From the *Tools* menu, select *Load from Audio Source*; this option will now have a tick next to it.

4. *Spectaculator* is now expecting audio input from your PC's Line-in socket. Connect this socket to your cassette recorder's EAR socket. *Spectaculator* recommends a mono to stereo lead for this, although I've personally found a standard Spectrum mono cable to work fine. You might need to experiment.

5. In Tasword, go to the main menu by pressing SymbolShift-A (right-shift and A on *Spectaculator*). Press L to load a file and ENTER to confirm. If you know the name of your file, type it now, otherwise just press enter and Tasword will load the first file it finds on the tape. Remember - you're loading from tape now; an emulated Spectrum on a PC is no better at reading tape data than the real thing, so you might well need to fiddle about with the volume settings to get a successful load.

6. As soon as the file's loaded successfully, Tasword brings it up on the screen. Press Symbol Shift-A to go back to the main menu, P for print and then ENTER to confirm. On the next screen, press ENTER several times to get to the bottom of the list and then one final time to proceed. Tasword should display a brief printing message and then return to the main editing screen with your text loaded.

7. To check that the process has worked, open up Notepad and navigate to your text file (C:\RS232.txt in this case). Now you're ready to start editing.

Other peripherals

Other than printers and joystick interfaces, there were many other peripherals designed for the Spectrum, an increasing number of which are supported by emulators today. *Spectaculator's* emulated peripheral hardware list is very impressive:

- *AMX and Kempston mouse.* Once activated, your PC mouse will take over the mouse in the Spectrum program being used. Not many Spectrum titles incorporated mouse control, however.

- Romantic Robot *Multiface* (all variants). A peripheral interface that could freeze the Spectrum at the press of a button, allowing the user to save this 'snapshot' to tape so that they could save their progress in a game. You could also modify the Spectrum's memory via this device, so it made entering POKEs for infinite lives (which were regularly published in the monthly Spectrum magazines) a great deal easier.

- *Cheetah SpecDrum.* An electronic drum set for the Spectrum (that came with its own software).

- *Currah μSpeech.* A speech synthesizer for the Spectrum which allowed you to run together allophones (speech sounds) and give your Spectrum a (Stephen Hawking-esque) voice. Something in the region of 50 games actually supported the *μSpeech*, including such classics as *Jetman*, although no game could possibly come close to the joy of achieving the best pronunciation of a swear word in Spectrum BASIC.

- *The Fuller AY Box* and the *Melodik AY-3-8912 Soundbox.* Both of these were peripherals for the 48K Spectrum which gave it improved sound capabilities – again, rarely exploited by commercial software.

- *The MGT/Datel Plus D interface.* The Plus D was possibly the most successful of the external disk drive interfaces and allowed you to connect a floppy disk drive to the Spectrum. See more about this below.

Meanwhile, *SPIN* emulates:

- *Kempston mouse.*

- The *Magnum Lightgun.* This was a peripheral produced by Amstrad that plugged into a BT-style socket on the back of the +2A and +3. It was bundled with certain promotional editions of the Spectrum, such as the '007 Action Pack' and wasn't really supported by subsequent commercial software. Enabling the lightgun in *SPIN* allows your mouse to take control of the crosshairs on these games - it's not quite the same as the feel of the gun in your hands, but for damn sure it's a great deal more accurate!

- The Romantic Robot *Multiface.*

- The *Cheetah SpecDrum.*

Fig 3.4 The Magnum Lightgun, emulated by ZX SPIN.

- The *Fuller AY Box* and the *Melodik AY-3-8912 Soundbox*

- *Currah μSpeech.*

- The *Expandor SoftROM.* An add-on that enabled programmers to page out the Spectrum's 16K ROM, effectively turning the Spectrum into a true 64K computer.

- The *MGT/Datel Plus D interface.*

- The DivIDE hard disk interface (see Chapter Eight).

The MGT Plus D interface

Released in 1988 by *Miles Gordon Technology* (MGT), the Plus D was a disk interface that allowed you to connect to your Spectrum pretty much any of the standard disk drives of the day. The interface was the successor by about two years to MGT's magnificent Disciple interface (a rival to the Sinclair Interface 1 which sat underneath the Spectrum - just like the IF1 - and also could connect to most standard disk drives as well as boasting ZX Net compatibility) and included also a 'magic' snapshot button and a parallel printer interface. It was compatible with most software designed for the Disciple and - due to the Disciple's own heritage - ZX microdrives. The original Plus D was black; the interface was later bought up by Datel and re-clad in a beige case.

Fig 3.5 The Plus D in its Datel case. The little red button froze the Spectrum so you could save a snapshot of your game to disk.

The Plus D was more than just another disk interface. The functionality of a Spectrum 128/+2 fitted with a Plus D system (interface and disk drive) far exceeded the functionality offered by the other main upgrade route for Spectrum owners at the time - the Spectrum +3. And upgrading to a Plus D was cheaper. At the start of 1989, for example, a +3 with a *Multiface 3* (a peripheral for the +3 by *Romantic Robot* with its own 'magic button' for creating snapshots files - the +3 itself came with nothing like this) would have cost you £245; a Plus D system was faster, larger (up to 780k), had a much more sophisticated OS, was more compatible with existing Spectrum software than the +3 was, and cost just £140. The sheer power of a Plus D system, therefore, made it extremely popular with those who owned it. Although it was not widely commercially supported, a very loyal user-base evolved; the system was supported by the long running Format Magazine of the INDUG user group.

The Plus D uses a very straightforward syntax; the main thing to remember is that LOAD and SAVE commands are suffixed by either d1 or d2 depending on which of two possible drives you are accessing. Thus:

```
LOAD d1 "squares"
SAVE d2 "squares" LINE 10
VERIFY d2 "squares"
ERASE d1 "squares"
CAT 1
```

If you're in 128K BASIC, the way in which the screen clears after you do a CAT command can get pretty irritating if you're wanting to load in a program you just saw listed on the disk. From 128K BASIC, bring up the *Options* menu (press shift and 1 together) then select *Screen*. This will return you to 128K BASIC, but in a mode where the screen doesn't clear in this way.

Although the Plus D/Disciple pretty much refuses to work in physical conjunction with a Sinclair Interface 1, you can use the IF 1's microdrive syntax in preference to the syntax above, so that programs modified to work on a microdrive should also work on a Plus D formatted disk. Thus:

```
LOAD D1 "zxf"    could be typed as    LOAD *"m";1;"zxf"
SAVE D2 "zxf"    could be typed as:   SAVE *"m";2;"zxf"
```

Snapshot files are denoted by an 'S' suffix for a 48K snapshot and a 'K' for a 128K snapshot, ie:

```
LOAD D1 "squares" S
LOAD D1 "squares128" K
```

There are two file formats for Plus D disk images: .IMG and .MGT, both of which are supported by *ZX SPIN* and *Spectaculator*. Although the Plus D was not widely supported by commercially released software, a number of adventure games were released on the format (most notably by *Zenobi Software*) plus it was also used by the electronic magazines *AlchNews* and *Outlet*. All of these disks, plus a number of other titles besides, can be downloaded from *The TZX Vault's* Plus D page at *www.tzxvault.org/plusd.htm*.

To enable the Plus D interface in *ZX SPIN*, select *Tools > Options > Hardware > Peripherals* and check the *MGT +D* box. To insert a disk image, select *File > Insert Disks* and then click on one of the folder icons at the end of the drive name to navigate to a file. *SPIN* comes with G+DOS (MGT's disk operating system) preloaded, so you can start typing in commands to the system straight away. A draw-back to *SPIN's* implementation, however, is that it does not allow you to create blank disks.

To enable the Plus D interface in *Spectaculator,* select *Tools > Options > Hardware* and check the *MGT/Datel Plus D Disk Interface* box. To insert a disk image, select *File > Open* and navigate to your file. *Spectaculator* does allow you to create a new disk; to do so, choose *File > New > Plus D disk image.* With *Spectaculator,* you'll need to create a system disk using the *Plus D System Tape* (available from the WoS website) before you can start typing in disk commands. Create a blank disk in the drive, then insert the tape into the virtual cassette player and load it. Follow the instructions and the program will format a system disk for you. To load the system from this disk, go to spectrum BASIC and just type RUN (and enter) with this disk in the drive.

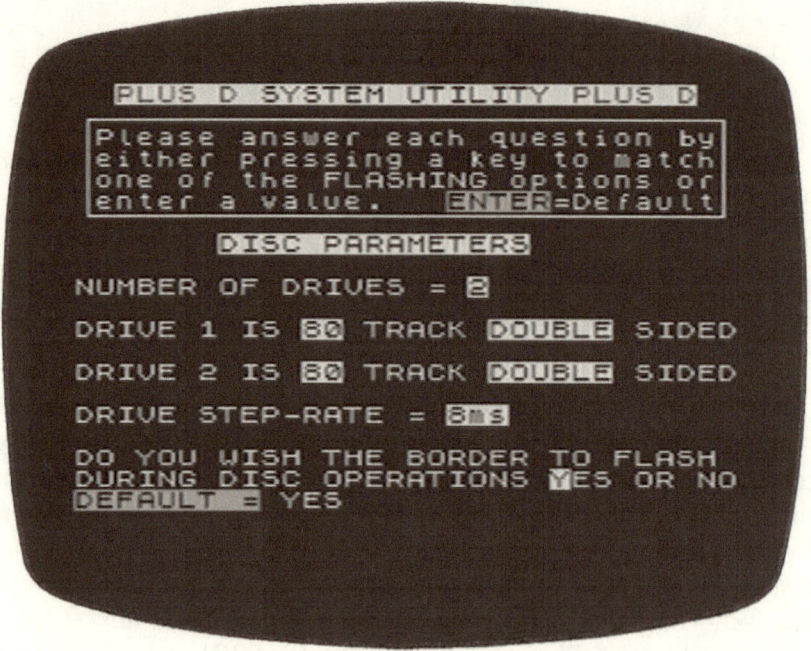

Fig 3.6 The Plus D System Tape running on Spectaculator. Just accept all the default values for your disk drive; answer no for the printer question that follows this screen, however, to avoid a lengthy printer questionnaire.

Spectaculator's Plus D emulation is very powerful and includes support for Uni-DOS (an enhanced DOS for the Plus D) as well as G+DOS, plus support for the interface's printer port (you can redirect it, just as we did for the RS232 output earlier in the Tasword walkthrough). Also, *Spectaculator* can read, write and format actual physical Plus D 3.5 inch floppy disks provided you are running it on Windows XP and using a standard 3.5 inch internal floppy disk drive (ie, *not* a floppy drive that connects via USB). So if you used to use this system and still have some disks in a box in the roof, their data might yet still be retrievable.

Television display

Of course, there was one vital piece of hardware that got plugged into your Spectrum that we've so far overlooked: your television set. Connected in the vast majority of cases via the good old RF cable, your telly received its signal from the computer in much the same way as it did an analogue TV signal (not that we called it 'analogue' in those days, of course). Anyone at the time who imagined that to mean crisp, razor sharp edges to pixelated objects was in for a sore disappointment: the Spectrum display was in most cases ghosted and a little blurred, and when sound got added to the TV signal with the 128K models (where previously there had only been the Speccy's own internal beeper), tuning just got worse: achieving non-distorted sound *and* the best available picture was nothing short of an art-form.

The early Spectrum emulators – and, in fact, some of the more recent ones which focus more on software development features and new, 'homebrew' hardware emulation – simply gave the pure Spectrum output as its display: here was the Spectrum image as it would have been displayed in the 80s if any of us had had the money to fork out for a proper monitor instead of using the old black-and-white TV on a chest of drawers in someone's bedroom. My first reaction to this was that it looked pretty damned impressive. But Spectrum emulation isn't just about making the Spectrum experience the best that it can *technically* be; there's a whole load of teenage nostalgia embedded in our associations with this machine and many of us miss those artefacts of low-tech gaming that came with the whole experience.

Loading tones is one such artefact. As you'll probably have noticed by now, a virtual cassette file can be 'flashloaded' in an instant, so waiting three to four minutes for a 48K game to load in is no longer required. If Spectrum emulation is just about getting to the games, why even have it as an option? But the wait – much as, in those days, we dreamed of software loading instantly – was part of the experience and the sound games made as they screeched their way – byte by torturous byte – into the Spectrum's memory became a part of the soundtrack to our lives. Such is the degree of familiarity Spectrum owners have with that sound, many (myself included) can instantly recognise it if ever it should be used as a sound effect in a film or TV programme (Star Trek IV moment after first timewarp, anyone?).

And loading tones nostalgia doesn't end with just the pure, unmolested digital tones of a hypothetically perfect Spectrum; as mentioned in Chapter One, *ZX SPIN* even includes an option to introduce tape hiss and wobble to loading tones – even to the extent that games won't load properly sometimes – just like they used to sound coming from a C90 tape of copied games (which, of course, you'll only have heard about from your unscrupulous mates; not something you've ever actually experienced yourself...).

The inconveniences of then are the fond memories of now; so it is too with TV display. I can't remember which emulator it was that first fiddled with display to achieve something a little more TV-realistic, but I'm pretty sure this was just achieved by making the display a little blurred. Then scan lines got added. Mike Wynne's wonderful *EightyOne* was I think the first emulator to introduce ghosting. Whilst excellent TV emulation is provided in *ZX SPIN* and *Spectaculator* now, it is in my opinion still Mike's emulator that wins the gold medal in this case: all manner of noise can be introduced to the display in *EightyOne*, including ghosting, dot crawl and – wonderfully – picture roll.

To play with the display features in *ZX SPIN*, go to *Tools > Options > Display*. *SPIN*'s main display features are blurring and scanlines. My own set-up uses OpenGL rendering with scanlines enabled at approximately 20%.

Spectaculator's display options are available via, select *View > Mimic TV Screen*, where you can also select scanlines (although you can't vary their intensity). Choosing Aerial (RF) Input will introduce a very satisfying ghosting to pixels. I also often use the

Black and White TV option for the full-flavour nostalgia experience. And you can learn more about *EightyOne* in Chapter Seven.

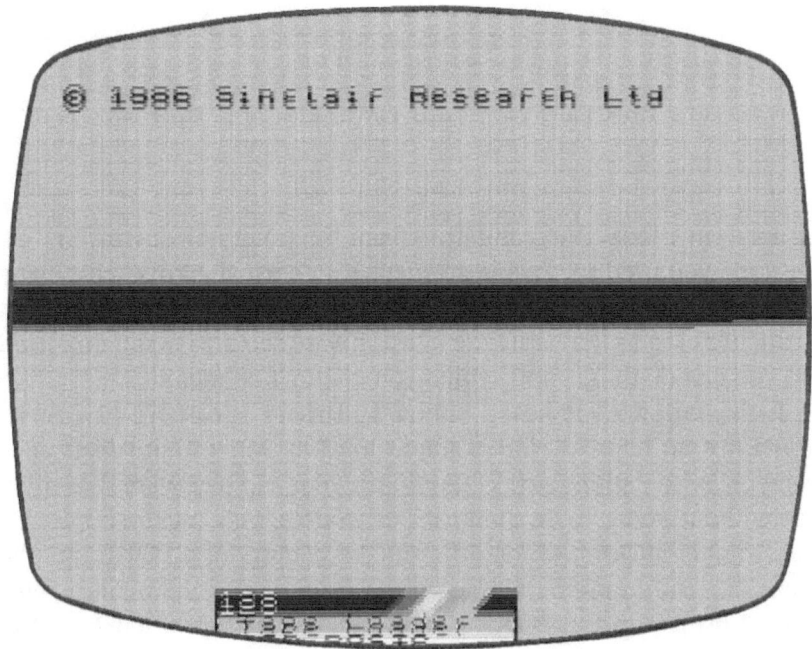

Fig 3.7 Mike Wynne's EightyOne comes complete with picture roll controls for added RF authenticity. Banging the side of your laptop display is not yet recognised as an input method.

Chapter Four
Emulator extras

So far we've looked at emulation from the point of view of how all the stuff you used to do is implemented in 'virtual' terms. But many emulators also have additional features - they offer you tools which are in addition to the hardware and software features being emulated (so you can do things now which you couldn't do then).

Let's start with Pokes. Although, strictly speaking, of course, POKEing an address, for example to give you infinite lives in a game, *was* something you could do on your old hardware, but often not without going to an awful lot of trouble. It's much simpler on Spectrum emulators, which offer the direct entry of a POKE into the game currently running via an option from one of the main menus. Ctrl+P brings up the POKE box on *Spectaculator,* where you can enter the memory location in the top box and the value you want that location to hold in the bottom. *ZX SPIN* has a whole POKE system available from *Tools > Poke memory,* which includes search access to *The Tipshop (www.the-tipshop.co.uk),* the largest on-line collection of hints, POKEs and tips for Spectrum games (maintained by Gerard Sweeney and Nick Humphries).

Input recording

Of course written hints and tips on how to get through games are a poor substitute for actually seeing it done. Previously this involved finding a suitably skilled friend and peering over his/her (ok - let's be honest - probably *his*) shoulder.

The modern equivalent of this is *input recording*, the function of which is to record all the things you do whilst using your emulated Spectrum for future playback (key presses and joystick waggles, that is; they don't record brewing a cup of tea whilst waiting for a game to load or cheering on the little matchstick men in Football Manager). When you do play back the recording, the emulated Spectrum will appear to work all by itself - as though instructed by an invisible user - replicating your every move in the game you recorded. In this way a personal best performance can be kept for posterity and shared around for others to learn from.

Apart from self-admiration and helping out a friend in need, input recording is used on an annual basis for the *Speccy Games Tournament,* in which ZX enthusiasts compete against each other for the highest score on a selected range of titles. Usually an 'official' snapshot file of each of the games is prepared by the competition administrator and distributed to all participants, who then play the games and submit the input recordings they made whilst doing so; it's a fair, reasonably non-corruptible, way of ensuring everybody is competing on a level playing field and that nobody can pass off grossly exaggerated figures as their own high score. It also allows players to learn from others' successes.

The two main input recording file formats are .AIR and .RZX, with the latter introduced as the successor to the former. The problem with AIR files was that they could only be played back on the specific emulator that created them: this meant in the past that all competitors in games tournaments had to use the same emulator (usually *RealSpectrum* – see the Chapter Seven); even if your own preferred emulator supported AIR file recording, one created by another emulator would not work. RZX, on the other hand, works *across* emulators, so all emulators which support this format should be able to run any RZX file created by any emulator - even an emulator running on a different platform. .AIR is now considered an obsolete format and is only supported by older emulators.

Working with RZX files

1. To record an RZX file in *Spectaculator*, first load the game you would like to play.

2. Select *Control > Action Replay (RZX) > Record.* Give your RZX file a name.

3. Play the game!

4. To play back your recording at a later date, again make sure the game itself is first of all loaded.

5. Select *Control > Action Replay (RZX) > Play*. Select the recording you made previously.

6. Sit back and watch the replay of your greatest ever triumph...

ZX SPIN's input recording works in exactly the same way. To record, select *Recording > Input (RZX) > Record RZX File* and give your file a name. Stop recording via *Recording > Stop recording*. And, to play back your creation, select *Recording > Input (RZX) > Play Back RZX File* and navigate to the desired RZX file.

Audio/Video

Input recording is fine if you want to show off to friends with a Spectrum emulator installed on their computer, but it is just possible, of course, that you might want something more portable that can play on a computer *without* such software installed. .AVI and .WAV files are - as you are no doubt already aware - standard Windows formats for video and audio respectively, and both are supported by *Spectaculator*. They're certainly not the most efficient of file formats for these purposes, but an advantage of recording in these formats is that the files created will play on much older PCs than the current 'standard.' Of course, you can always use additional tools to convert them into other formats (you could even encode and burn them onto a DVD if you so desired and watch them on your TV – there's full circle for you – so then the recipient of your recording wouldn't even have to own a computer, let alone a Spectrum emulator).

You Tube is awash with Spectrum videos. These are usually walkthroughs of games created with audio commentaries, however there have been much more innovative Spectrum video projects also. Probably the best example of this is Nick Humphries' series of *Your Sinclair Rock 'n' Roll Years* documentaries, each taking a year of the Spectrum's life (from 1982 to 1990), set to a soundtrack of music from that year (there's even a Christmas special). You can download these very high quality videos (or follow YouTube links) from *www.ysrnry.co.uk/tvprog*.

Audio and video recording are both located on *Spectaculator's* 'Control' menu. Select *Control > Video Clip (AVI)* or *Control > Audio Recording (WAV)* and then click on *Record* to give your file a name and start recording it. *Control > Video Clip (AVI) / Audio Recording (WAV) > Stop* then – you guessed it – stops recording.

ZX SPIN has these options on its *Recording* menu and allows you to select a video recording compression format (so, if you have the DivX codec installed on your PC, for example, you can record in that format without having to do a separate conversion). This can be set up via *Recording > Video > Configure Output*.

Graphics

If all that sounds a bit too exotic for your needs and you just want to capture a screen or two to put on a web page or email to a friend, there are, of course, options on most emulators to create standard Windows graphics files. Quite a number allow you to save screenshots as .BMP (Windows bitmap) files for editing in a standard graphics package and just recently BMP export has also been created for the *ZX Printer,* so you can now print from your emulated Spectrum to an emulated ZX Printer and save the printer's output as a BMP file.

To save a screenshot from *Spectaculator,* simply click on the save icon (or select *File > Save As*) and choose *Spectrum Screenshot (.bmp)* from the filetype list). To save printer output, click on the save icon in the top-left corner of the printer output window.

To save a screenshot from *ZX SPIN,* select *File > Save current screen* and type in your filename (*SPIN* will then ask you which file format you want to use – chose BMP or GIF). To save printer output, you need to click on the blank page icon that clears the printer window; *SPIN* will then ask you if you want to save the current output as a Windows bitmap.

And what about doing it the other way around - wouldn't it be cool to turn a Windows BMP into a Spectrum screen? *Z80,* the shareware Spectrum emulator by *Gerton Lunter,* has offered a BMP import feature for several years now, although the control this option offers you is quite limited. A much better way is to use an external program to turn your graphic into a Spectrum screen. The common file format developed for Spectrum screens is the *.SCR* format - drop an SCR into *Spectaculator* and the Spectrum screen created appears straight away (you could then save it out as a SCREEN$ to a cassette file). SCRs cannot be edited by standard Windows graphics packages, but there are a whole host of freeware programs that can. We'll explore these in the next chapter.

Other features

ZX SPIN and *Spectaculator* have some other features that are worth noting, in particular their built-in debuggers for tracing coding issues in machine code programs. *SPIN* also has a built-in assembler. Not being an assembly language programmer myself, I have no experience of using these features (nor opinion as to whether they're any good or not). Traditionally, however, machine code programming had to be done within Spectrum software; the advantages of a Windows tool built into an emulator, where code written can be directly tested, are obvious.

If you're already a Spectrum machine code programmer then you probably don't need to hear anything from me on the topic. If you're not and would like to become one, however, these tools might make this process a lot easier than it used to be. I recall that one of the bibles for this process back in the Spectrum's day was Melbourne House's *Spectrum Machine Language for the Absolute Beginner* (edited by William Tang). Scroll down to *Complete Books* on the WoS *Archive* page and you'll find a PDF version of this book to download.

Chapter Five
Utilities

So far our focus has been mostly on emulation. This will be the starting point for many of you returning to the Spectrum scene, and for many nothing further will be required. Fair enough. Many - not all - of the increasing number of PC utilities available for the Spectrum are targeted at the more serious Spectrum hobbyist - in particular those wanting more powerful tools with which to develop new Spectrum software than the Spectrum itself is able to provide; that's not the sort of thing likely to appeal to everyone. But this is not to say that this corner of the community is all about ultra-serious coding; far from it. Plenty of users like to use these programs just to help them create, for example, an entry for the annual *Crap Games Competition* organised initially by the members of the *comp.sys.sinclair* newsgroup (a competition inspired originally by the now infamous *Cascade Cassette 50* compilation of 50 quite appalling games). Programming, after all, was part of what the Spectrum was meant to be about, and an important aspect of its appeal today is the ease with which it's possible to create new programs compared to the complexity of creating programs on the PC. In this chapter, therefore, we'll take a brief look at the sorts of utility available to you should you start becoming interested in this sort of thing; I will be mentioning utilities by name, but I won't be getting too specific about the precise details of any particular utility - the nature of the scene is that these often tend to be developed very rapidly and then left for quite long periods before another burst of rapid development. Getting too specific here, therefore, will render the chapter out-of-date very quickly. Also, don't assume that the titles mentioned here are the *only* programs available - there are many that won't be mentioned simply because there are too many to go into, and it's also very likely that programs not conceived of at the time of writing will be taking the scene by storm by the time you read this. In most cases, I won't be giving out URLs either. Other than, of course, *www.worldofspectrum.org/utilities.html*. The majority of utilities mentioned here are available from that page.

Towards the end of the last chapter we were looking at graphics, this seems like a good place to start in our exploration of PC utilities. In the last chapter we looked very briefly at the SCR file format as a means of storing a Spectrum screen display on your PC and there are plenty of utilities to help you work with these without having to go anywhere near an emulator. Of course Windows doesn't recognise SCR files as a valid graphics format (funnily enough, Windows wasn't written with Spectrum emulation in mind), so don't expect *Windows Explorer* to displays these as pretty little thumbnails. The very first thing you'll need therefore if you have more than a couple of SCRs in a folder is a viewer program. These won't allow you to manipulate your graphics much, but they will let you look at them. A good example of such a program is *ZX Screens* by *Pavel Plíva*, a very simple screen viewer which will display a whole directory of SCR files one screen after another using the Slide Show option. Pavel, by the way, has a particular interest in grabbing Spectrum screens for the purpose of creating game maps and has produced other PC software dedicated to this purpose (*ZX Maps Creator*) as well as a website at which completed maps can be displayed (*http://maps.speccy.cz*).

In so far as actual manipulation is concerned, there are many titles to choose from. One of my personal favourites is *SevenuP* by *Jamie Tejedor Gomez* – put simply, a *Windows Paint* type application that produces SCRs rather than bitmaps. I've always found *SevenuP* a very usable and straightforward application. It perfectly emulates the Spectrum's graphics limitations whilst at the same time gives you a variety of useful drawing tools to use, enabling you to build up images very quickly without having to wonder how colour clash will mutilate them. Buttons allow you to select INK and PAPER colours, turn on/off FLASH and BRIGHT, and zoom in on your picture so that your individual pixels can be placed perfectly on character borders.

In case you'd forgotten, the Spectrum screen display is 256 pixels across by 192 pixels down. These are divided into 8 x 8 character cells called 'attribute blocks': 32 of them across and 24 of them down. Per individual attribute block, only two colours are permitted, one of them the INK colour and one of them the PAPER colour. So if in *SevenuP* you draw in an attribute block a little smiley face in red INK on yellow PAPER, then change your INK colour to blue and click on one of the eyes to change it, the whole smiley face will turn to blue against yellow rather than red against yellow since the INK value for the attribute has now been changed (from red to blue). There are eight colours to choose from (black is 0, dark blue is 1, red is 2, magenta is 3, green is 4, cyan is 5, yellow is 6 and white is 7), however these are *almost* doubled by using the BRIGHT option to produce brighter hues (only 'almost' because black is the same whether BRIGHT is on or off). Clever use of BRIGHT can make for very effective screens: BRIGHT white, for example, can make normal white appear an effective grey. Unfortunately, a single attribute can only be all BRIGHT or all not BRIGHT; you can't have some of the pixels in a character set to BRIGHT and others not.

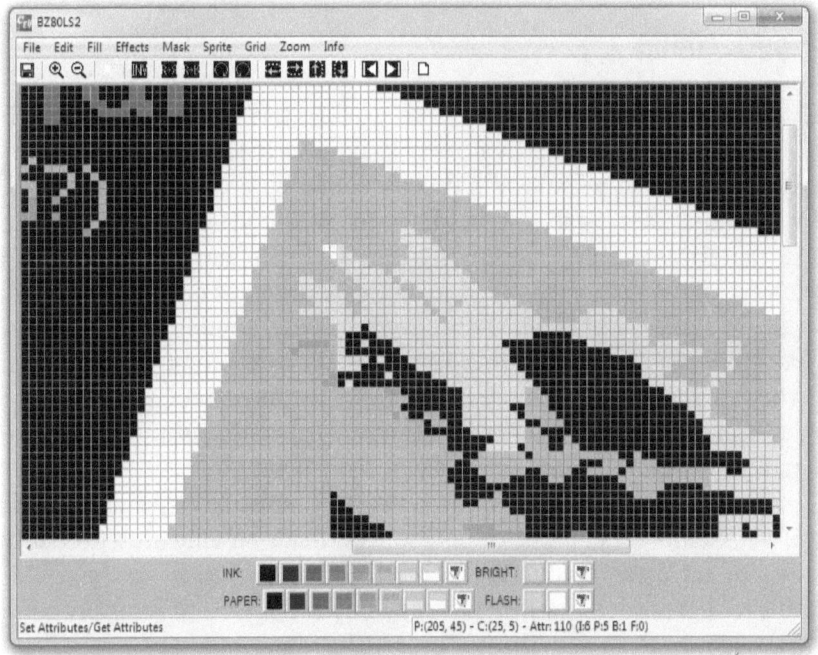

Fig 5.1 SevenuP's grid (which can be zoomed up to 48:1) allows precision pixel placement.

Other excellent graphics utilities can be found in the graphics editor section of Tony Thompson's *Tommy Gun*, in Claus Jahn's feature-packed *ZX-Paintbrush* (see *ZX-Modules* below) and in *BMP2SCR* by *LCD*. The latter utility's distinctiveness lies in its ability also to convert bitmap images into SCR files, allowing you effectively to take any image from your hard drive and turn it into a Spectrum screen. There are in fact a number of programs that do this (including the aforementioned *ZX Screens*), but *BMP2SCR* employs by far the largest number of conversion techniques to explore, each giving different results. One such approach, for example, is the black and white dithering of a colour bitmap. This has been explored also in Derek Jolly's *YASPIC* (Yet another Spectrum Image Convertor; this does not appear to be listed at WoS and can be obtained from *http://rivet.50megs.com/speccy.html*), which allows you to dither an image and then colour it in. Both *BMP2SCR* and *YASPIC* allow you to save your output as either an SCR graphics file or TAP cassette file.

Programming

Quite simply, Spectrum programming has never been easier than it is now, and this is due in no small part to the emergence of new utilities designed to help this process. Machine code programmers, for example, are now able to develop their code in their favourite text editor, assemble this directly to a TAP file and test it there and then on an emulator, thanks to a new generation of cross assemblers, such as *Pasmo* by Julián Albo. And many emulators (*SPIN* and *Spectaculator* included) have in-built debuggers for tracking down errors in the code being tested too. The most recent version of *SPIN*, in fact, even features its very own in-built assembler, so you need never leave the emulator if you don't want to.

For these particular tools to make any sense you'll still need to know assembly language, of course, and that's an elite club probably most of us don't belong to (myself included). But you can still achieve a great deal in the Spectrum's own BASIC. If your problem now becomes how to write better BASIC, therefore, then you have a treat in store: Paul Dunn's BASIC development tool *BASin*.

BASin, which started out life with the name 'SPIN Light' and visually resembled an emulator very closely, is a Windows ZX BASIC programming environment. Simply put, it enables you to program in Spectrum BASIC outside of an actual Spectrum and test your program within an embedded Spectrum emulator. The main editor window offers you the luxury of typing BASIC into a Windows style text editor whilst at the same time recognizing BASIC commands and highlighting code in the way a dedicated code editor would. Additional features include a dedicated UDG (User Defined Graphics) editor that allows you to create your UDGs by clicking on an 8x8 grid and then sends the code as line-by-line decimal entries to your BASIC listing and a screen graphics editor every bit as fully featured as *SevenuP*. The program also features in its help system the full original Spectrum BASIC programming manual. I love *BASin*. I think it's one of the most innovative PC applications within the Spectrum scene. You can see a worked example of a program I created with this application at the end of this chapter.

Of course, Spectrum programming does go beyond its BASIC. As mentioned earlier, *ZX SPIN* features its own built-in assembler to help you to write software in super-fast machine code. If assembly language is a bit too much of a jump for you, however, an in-between step of sorts is compiled BASIC. A BASIC compiler takes a BASIC program listing and converts it into machine code. If this sounds too good to be true, that's because it partly is: BASIC compiled into machine code is never as fast as things would have been if you'd written your program in assembly language in the first place. Also, compilers can be a little quirky in their interpretation of your program and you often need to rewrite bits of it to make it more easily digestible. So it's not a magic wand. That said, compiled BASIC *does* run faster, even if it's not as fast as pure machine code, and the time you spend optimizing your BASIC will still be a great deal less time than you would have had to spend learning assembly language.

Although *BASin* does have its own compiler, work on this feature – to the best of my knowledge – was not completed. Two other options remain. The first of these, *ZX BASIC* compiler by Jose Rodriguez, can take your Spectrum BASIC program in a text file and compile it into machine code from the command prompt. This sounds incredibly daunting, but is actually fairly straightforward and the feedback given by the program when compiling fails is extremely useful (for example, when I tried to compile the 'Depth' BASIC program used in the example later on in this chapter, *ZX BASIC's* feedback indicated it was unhappy I'd called one of my variables 'sub', perhaps because this could be confused with 'GO SUB' commands).

My top tip for this application, if you download and run the executable setup file (which you can obtain from the *ZX BASIC* site: *www.boriel.com/software/the-zx-basic-compiler/?lang=en*), is *not* to install it in the suggested Program Files folder. For some reason, Windows 7 has difficulty believing me responsible enough to create or delete files in this folder and its children – even though I'm set up as administrator – and has to double check with me every time: this immensely annoying – and, quite frankly, condescending – habit breaks the *ZX BASIC* compiler process, making it impossible to create the output file. Install it instead in a new folder in C drive, which will also make it easier to navigate to later. Copy your BASIC program to this folder also (write it in a text editor such as notepad – alternatively, write it in *BASin* and then chose the *Edit > Copy Listing* option so you can paste it into a text editor – and save it in the format *filename.bas* – the '.bas' is really important or the file will get saved as a text file). From the Windows Start button, open up a command console (in the 'Search programs and files' box for Windows 7 or the Run box for XP, type 'Command' and hit return). Type 'CD\' and hit return, then 'CD ZX BASIC Compiler' to enter the folder for the application. To run the compiler, then type in 'zxb filename.bas –t –B'. If the compile is successful, you'll see in the folder a brand new .TAP file which you can load straight into an emulator. Once it's loaded, activate the machine code with a PRINT USR statement – take a look in the tape browser for your emulator and note down the first of the two numbers (this is the start address of the program) after the first 'Bytes' file name, then type into your Spectrum 'PRINT USR [that number]'. Your sparkly machine code program should now run. For more about using this program, see *www.boriel.com/wiki/en/index.php/ZX_BASIC:Zxb*

The second option is to use an actual Spectrum compiler – exactly as you would have back in the eighties. The best known compiler for the Spectrum is HiSoft's BASIC compiler. We'll take a closer look at this in the worked example later on in the chapter.

AGD/PGD/SEUD

Special mention is worth making here of Jonathan Cauldwell's *Arcade Games Designer (AGD)* and other game design tools

Platform Games Designer (PGD; you can read a review of this in Appendix B) and *Shoot 'Em Up Designer (SEUD).* These actually aren't PC utilities at all, but recent Spectrum programs for designing games in a variety of well-established formats. *AGD* in particular has become quite popular within the community in recent years – perhaps because it's free (*PGD* and *SEUD* are both paid for titles available from Cronosoft) – and has led to a number of new titles being developed with it. A few of these, in fact, are packaged with the iOS version of *Spectaculator* (see Chapter Nine). Back in Christmas 2006, I wrote a game with my son, Jack, using *PGD* called *Elvin the Elf;* proper good fun it was too.

Fig 5.2 Elvin the Elf. My contribution to Spectrum platform gaming.

SpecBAS

Back to Paul Dunn. Both *ZX SPIN* and *BASin* are projects he no longer maintains. Dunny's current Spectrum project is something even bigger and more imaginative than *BASin* was: a new operating system for a PC based on Sinclair BASIC. The ultimate goal for *SpecBAS* – which is available from *www.specbas.co.uk,* complete with a very comprehensive user manual – is that it will run on a PC all by itself, acting both as an operating system and a programming language. Perfect for that old laptop you have lying around.

Why create such a system? I remember when I first encountered a PC being bemused that you couldn't just program it – like we did the Spectrum – without first having to load a program with a programming language on it. In recent years there's been something of a growing interest in the importance of simple computers that people can learn more easily to program on, something we lost sight of as computers became increasingly complicated and driven by products rather than programming. In the UK, developments reflecting this include the current government's plans to put programming at the heart of the IT curriculum and the high profile release of the *Raspberry Pi* computer.

Writing on their website about their reasons for creating the *Raspberry Pi*, its designers claim they were concerned about the decline in the numbers and skills of students applying to university to study Computer Science:

> Something had changed the way kids were interacting with computers. A number of problems were identified: the colonisation of the ICT curriculum with lessons on using Word and Excel, or writing webpages; the end of the dot-com boom; and the rise of the home PC and games console to replace the Amigas, BBC Micros, Spectrum ZX and Commodore 64 machines that people of an earlier generation learned to program on. www.raspberrypi.org/about

As a learning device, therefore, a simple computer with its own programming language is a very useful thing. Not all computers have to be state-of-the-art. BASIC, after all, is a *Beginners* All-purpose Symbolic Instruction Code: it's intended as a language that helps people to acquire skills.

Just to be clear, *SpecBAS* is not a Spectrum emulator. Although it's based on Sinclair BASIC, Dunny's work has already expanded this well beyond the limitations of the original (not being restricted to 16K probably helped quite a bit). In its present state of development, it's not an operating system yet either. But you can download it as a PC application. And it's rather good.

On loading up, *SpecBAS* does look rather like a Spectrum screen, albeit one with a much higher resolution. Straight away, you can test out its BASIC credentials by typing in that 'Hello World' program, ie:

```
10  PRINT "Hello"
20  GOTO 10
```

Type RUN (and hit enter) and your first ever *SpecBAS* program runs, exactly like it used to be. As well as a manual giving information about all the instructions available to you, there are also a number of demonstration programs packaged with the download.

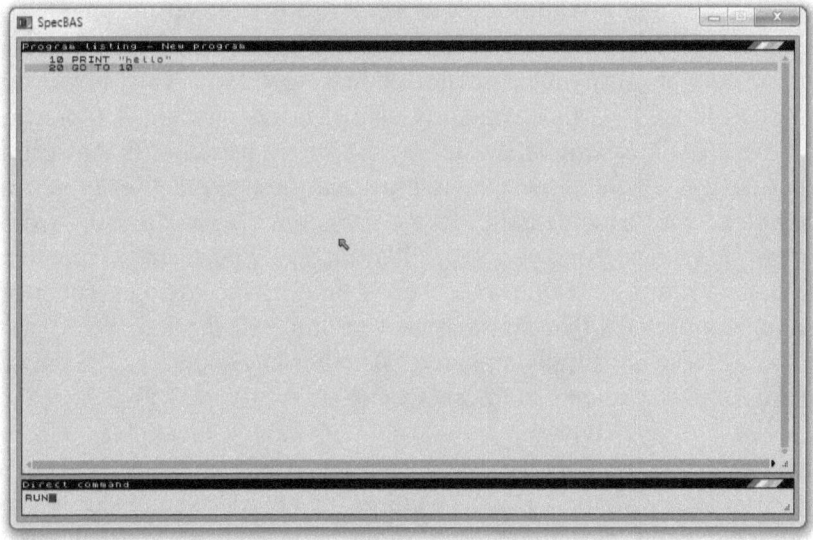

Fig 5.3 SpecBAS waits for the enter key to be pressed.

I got a little confused about the demonstration programs at first; I couldn't work out how to get to them from within *SpecBAS*. When I then actually read the manual (scroll through until you get to the bit about LOAD and SAVE – currently titled 'Fun with the Filesystem' – and read the introductory paragraphs) and learned that *SpecBAS* creates its own folder in your Windows user account and *SpecBAS* can only look at programs and file within that folder. On my Windows 7 PC, that means I had to go to the folder at C:\Users\CW[that's my account]\specbas. Copy the demonstration programs from the folder they come in to that folder and you'll be able to see them just fine from within *SpecBAS*. CAT lists the contents of the current folder and you can load programs exactly like you used to: ie, LOAD "Program name". I recommend the program 'Circles'; it's groovy.

Sound

The Spectrum beeper was so famously bad that many seem to recall it as a feature of all Spectrums, rather than just the original Spectrum and the Spectrum plus. Of course, with the Spectrum 128 came our very own three Channel AY chip and with it a whole new level of musical possibilities was added to the Spectrum scene. To listen to an AY tune you would ordinarily have to load up the game it was part of onto your emulator or real Spectrum. Now, however, you can listen to it independently using an independent AY player. *AY-3-8910/12 Emulator* by Sergey Bulba is particularly powerful because it not only allows you to play ready-made AY files (you can download these, incidentally, from WoS), but also to rip them from snapshot or tape files yourself. It's not just Spectrum *games* that contain AY music, by the way; there's an ever-increasing number of demo soundtracks that you can also get hold of through WoS, and some of these are simply amazing. Another key source of ZX music is *http://zxtunes.com*. A more recent alternative to *AY-3-8910/12 Emulator* by vitamin_caig is *ZXtune,* available from *http://code.google.com/p/zxtune/*

After many years, I'm still waiting for an AY sequencer in the *piano roll* style (used by PC midi sequencers such as *Cakewalk*) that generates AY output and can be saved either as an AY file or a TAP file. This would be really, really useful. As it is, there are plenty of tools with which to create AY music, but these follow the *Tracker* method of interface originally devised within Spectrum software itself for sequencing AY tunes, and this is a little complex, to say the least (see, for example, *Vortex Tracker II*, also by Sergey Bulba). Using these tools, however, some fantastic tunes have been created over the last few years, and not just for games and demos either. Multi-national group *AY Riders* have so far released four whole albums of music using the Spectrum's AY chip (you can download the albums from their site - *http://ay-riders.speccy.cz* - for free and in MP3 format) - they've even gigged live in Poland in front of 200 odd people using real Spectrums (and lots of them).

Of course, Spectrum sound isn't only about music. All those little burps, whistles and gurgles produced by the Spectrum beeper each time you died/acquired an object/killed a minion required their own work too. Shiru's lovely little beeper sound utility, *BeepFX* (*http://shiru.untergrund.net/software.shtml*) now takes all the pain out of this job, allowing you to play with and string together sequences of Spectrum sound effects until you've found exactly the thing you're looking for. There's an AY sound effects generator available from the same page also – *AYFX Editor* – a video of which can be seen at *www.youtube.com/watch?v=XI6aW2QSUXw*

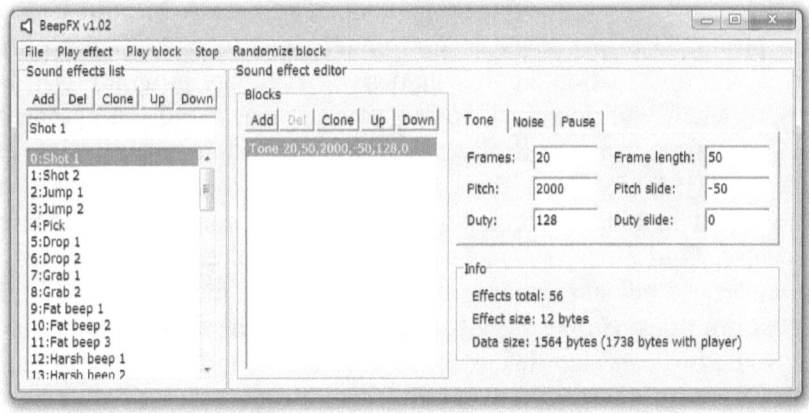

Fig 5.4 BeepFX comes with a demo file full of sounds to play with.

Organising your games/research

Not all PC Spectrum utilities are about developing new Spectrum software. Some simply aim to help you organise the software you already have on your hard disk. Via the *World of Spectrum* website, after all, you now have access to literally thousands of Spectrum titles for your emulator (or real Spectrum) - more than you could ever have imagined yourself having back in the 80s - and sifting through even a small percentage of these on your PC can be an overwhelming process. Personally, I prefer just sorting all the games into folders by publisher (this could also be done by author), but this is a rather long and arduous process (and requires a somewhat anal mentality towards hard disk organization – which I happen to have). *Spectaculator* offers a 'favourites' menu, which you can organise just like your *Internet Explorer* favourites (so the files themselves can stay in a single folder), but this too has to be set up in the first place. Also, neither of these options gives you any additional information *about* the games (ie, author, publisher, year of release and so on; although you could, of course, edit this information into file/folder titles).

A number of games database programs exist, however, which you can use to help you sort all this out. Perhaps the most well-known of these within the Spectrum community is WoS maintainer *Martijn van der Heide*'s 'Spectrum Games Database' (SGD). A DOS program now no longer maintained (although Martijn Groen has produced a Windows version called *WinSGD*), *SGD* not only gives you information on your games (the database program itself is empty when you download it, but you can download pre-prepared database files from WoS along with the program), but also link to the actual files on your system, display their loading screens and allow you to launch them in an emulator of your choice. More recently, *Paul Thompson* has taken the universal emulator front-end *Gamebase* and customised it with a ready-made database of Spectrum titles. *Gamebase* ZX, then, performs the same sorts of task as SGD, but can also link to Inlay card scans and instructions text files. It's also a Windows program.

It's worth bearing in mind that - as a research tool - the WoS website itself is just as comprehensive as either of these utilities. Often the sheer size of the WoS archive eclipses the immense power of the internal database and search engine, custom-built for the site. Clicking on a game title will often throw up links to the game's inlay card, instructions, advertisements for the game, reviews of the game in any of the Spectrum magazines and hints/tips/pokes/maps for the game (linking into the *Tipshop*'s database) as well as the actual game file itself. All titles within the archive can also be played on-line using the excellent *ZZ Spectrum* Java emulator (which runs in a web page, so you don't even have to have an emulator installed on your computer). Clicking on the title's author will usually throw up a list of other titles by the same author (each of which can be clicked and explored in the same way); clicking on the title's publisher will usually throw up a list of other titles by the same publisher... and so on. A ratings system has been introduced for all titles and you are encouraged to contribute your own ratings so that an increasingly representative indication of how popular the title is can be developed. The complexity of the system (never mind the content) is mind-boggling, and it's unlikely that any off-line database will ever come close to matching it.

It's not just *WoS* that offers a lot of structured information either. Plenty more websites generate a great deal of information about various different aspects of the machine and its influence. As the amount of on-line, Spectrum related information continues to grow, it's becoming increasingly difficult to find any one particular piece of information amongst it all. And that's why Gerard Sweeney invented the *Speccy Search Bar* for Internet Explorer and other web browsers. Install it and you get a little search box in your browser's tool bar that searches many of the sites listed in Appendix A. A real time saver.

ZX-Modules

There's an important suite of Windows Spectrum applications which so far I haven't mentioned, largely because it fits into so many categories. PC Spectrum software development has generally slowed down in the years since I wrote the first edition of this book: in part, this is because many of the applications are about as fully featured as they're going to get (there are only so many bells and whistles that can be added to, for example, a Spectrum paint program); in part it's because tablets and other mobile devices are now a key area for new software development. The *ZX-Modules* suite by Claus Jahn, however, is one of the few PC applications still under development and it's huge. The suite consists of a number of modules, each with their own dedicated function covering many of the areas discussed so far in this chapter. These are (descriptions taken from Claus' website at *www.zxmodules.de*):

- ZX-Central (not yet released). Manages your favourite ZX-Spectrum programs (emulators and tools); binds any Windows-compatible ZX-Spectrum program into a panel; lets you design layouts; helps you updating your programs and tools

- ZX-Explorer. Opens or displays ZX-Spectrum emulator files on drives, also detects programs/games automatically. Can also be used as a thumbnail viewer. It manages also the display of compressed files.

- ZX-Favourites. Stores most wanted programs with their game information in a database. Can import S.G.D. and other databases.

- ZX-Preview. Shows screen$, basic listings, system variables, etc. of ZX-Spectrum emulator files.

- ZX-Blockeditor. Edits the blocks of ZX-Spectrum emulator files [a *block* is a part of a cassette file; most files are made out of two blocks - the header (the bit that announces the name of the file) and the main code], e.g. all TZX format blocks. Create DSK or TRD disk image files.

- ZX-Editor. Edits ZED-files and many more ZX-Spectrum emulator files directly. Contains ZX-BASIC and BETABASIC syntax checker and syntax help. Lets you run your edited file.

- ZX-Paintbrush. Graphic editor. Edits Spectrum screen$ and other picture formats. Also Multi-block editing for tape and disk image files is supported. Lets you run your edited file.

- ZX-Gamestatistics (not yet released). Comples scanning Spectrum archives and building statistics about similarities of the games.

- ZX-Assembler (not yet released). A complete Assembler/Disassembler system.

The modules published so far are very feature-rich pieces of software, well worth the wait for their release. *ZX-Paintbrush,* for example, is packed with features, my personal favourite being the ability to create text for your Spectrum pictures using any of your installed Windows fonts. At the time of its release, this was the first Spectrum graphics editor that allowed this and I was very excited by it! *ZX-Blockeditor* is also an extremely competent piece of software, which we will look at in the worked example at the end of the chapter.

Tape utilities

One final category of utility worth looking at is utilities for working with and creating cassette files. As discussed earlier, a .TAP or .TZX file is actually an emulated cassette, if you will, containing any number of actual Spectrum programs. Emulators like *SPIN* and *Spectaculator* that have a separate cassette recorder window list those files on the tape in the order that they come. Beyond looking at these files, however, there's not much more that you can do with them - other than load them, of course - and whilst that's fine in the vast majority of cases, there are occasions when being able to delete individual files from the tape or change the order that they play in could come in handy.

The undisputed king of cassette file manipulation was originally WoS maintainer *Martijn van der Heide*'s 'Taper'. In addition to letting you play around with the individual files on a tape, *Taper* also lets you copy files between tapes, play tapes out to a real Spectrum and turn input from a cassette recorder plugged into your PC into a TZX file. *Taper* is still a powerful program to use, however - like Martijn's *Spectrum Games Database* - it's a DOS only program that can experience problems on modern PCs.

Tape Explorer, for example, is a great little Windows program by *Dan Fry* that allows you to move and delete files on a Spectrum cassette in pretty much exactly the way I described earlier. This utility only works with TAP files, however. *Spectrum Tape Loader* by *Jocelyn Gibart* offers similar functionality with both TAP *and* TZX files, although this allows you to move *blocks* rather than whole files, making the process slightly more complex for the beginner. Claus Jahn's *ZX-Blockeditor* also performs this function. *Spectrum Tape Loader* takes input from a real cassette being played in through your PC's sound card, which it can then turn into a TZX or TAP file. I must admit that I personally have not had much success in using this particular utility for this purpose, however, whilst I have managed it with *MakeTZX* by *Ramsoft*.

You can, of course, make a new TZX file straight out of an emulator if you're creating programs of your own; TZX creation programs are aimed, of course, at the capture and preservation of *existing* games on cassette. Information stored on magnetic tape doesn't last forever, after all, so simply collecting the cassettes themselves isn't enough insofar as preservation is concerned. As the archive of games at WoS grows there are naturally less and less cassettes that haven't already been captured in this way, thanks to the extremely hard work of the few individuals who contribute to this project, namely Martijn van der Heide, Steve Brown, Andy Barker, Tony Barnett and Juan Pablo López-Grao. At the time of writing, however, there are still over 2,500 known Spectrum cassette titles not yet archived. These are the 'missing in action' (MIA) titles that have yet to be found and converted. They turn up in charity shops and car boot sales, and it's our job to find them!

Converting real cassettes into TZX files, however, has been likened to a black art that some achieve with ridiculous ease whilst others fail miserably at. This approach to conversion moved me from the latter to the former group. It might work for you too.

1 Connect your cassette recorder to your PC's Line-In socket. Fire up your favourite PC sound editor (if you don't have one, download Audacity for free from http://audacity.sourceforge.net/) and set up a new file: make the file 8 bit mono (not 16 bit). Press play on your cassette player and record on your sound editor. Save the resulting WAV file somewhere handy.

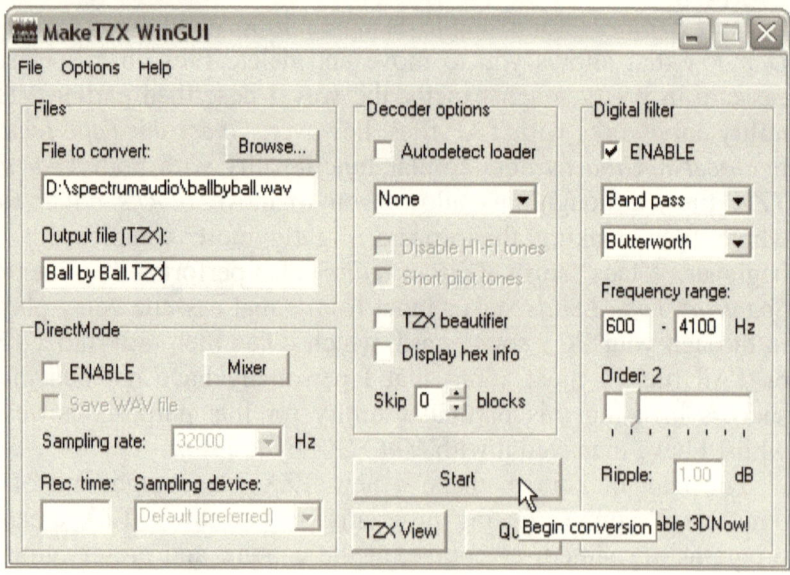

Fig 5.5 MakeTZX's main set-up panel.

2 Load up Ramsoft's 'MakeTZX' (download this application from

http://ramsoft.bbk.org.omegahg.com/maketzx.html and locate your WAV file. MakeTZX claims to be able to convert straight from your tape recorder using 'Direct Mode' (ie, no need to sample in a separate sound editor) but in practice this doesn't always work (probably a hardware issue). Enable the digital filter (see Figure 5.5 above) and press Start.

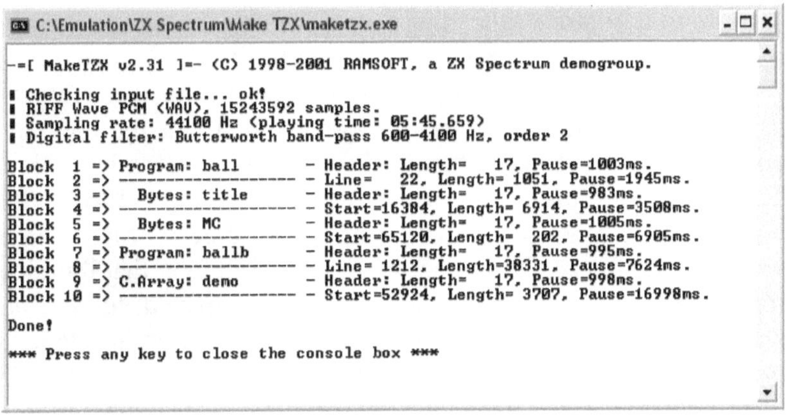

```
C:\Emulation\ZX Spectrum\Make TZX\maketzx.exe
-=[ MakeTZX v2.31 ]=- (C) 1998-2001 RAMSOFT, a ZX Spectrum demogroup.

! Checking input file... ok!
! RIFF Wave PCM (WAV), 15243592 samples.
! Sampling rate: 44100 Hz (playing time: 05:45.659)
! Digital filter: Butterworth band-pass 600-4100 Hz, order 2

Block  1 => Program: ball      - Header: Length=    17, Pause=1003ms.
Block  2 => ------------------ - Line=     22, Length= 1051, Pause=1945ms.
Block  3 =>   Bytes: title     - Header: Length=    17, Pause=983ms.
Block  4 => ------------------ - Start=16384, Length= 6914, Pause=3508ms.
Block  5 =>   Bytes: MC        - Header: Length=    17, Pause=1005ms.
Block  6 => ------------------ - Start=65120, Length=  202, Pause=6905ms.
Block  7 => Program: ballb     - Header: Length=    17, Pause=995ms.
Block  8 => ------------------ - Line=   1212, Length=38331, Pause=7624ms.
Block  9 => C.Array: demo      - Header: Length=    17, Pause=998ms.
Block 10 => ------------------ - Start=52924, Length= 3707, Pause=16998ms.

Done!
*** Press any key to close the console box ***
```

Fig 5.6 MakeTZX's output window.

3 Seconds later - if you're lucky - one TZX file to load into an emulator or submit to WoS for others to enjoy if it was MIA.

For more information, check out the Spectrum Tape Preservation Project web page at *www.worldofspectrum.org/stp/*

'Depth' – a worked example

Here's an example of a Spectrum game created using some of the utilities mentioned above. I wrote *Depth* in 2005 in response to a request for BASIC games from Cronosoft's Simon Ullyatt; he wanted to make a modern version of Cascade's *Cassette 50* (a games compilation so famously bad it not only inspired the annual *Crap Games Competition,* it even has its own Wikipedia entry; see *http://en.wikipedia.org/wiki/Cassette_50)* and sell copies of it for charity. I don't think the project – titled 'Cassette 50 Reloaded' – ever took off in the end (collating fifty new BASIC programs is quite a challenge). So here is my contribution. You can find the BASIC listing in Appendix C, by the way.

In *Depth*, the future has arrived in the manner of *Waterworld* and the whole planet is flooded. People now make their living by diving in mini submarines to collect scrap metal from the ocean – tractors, crashed helicopters, fallen spacecraft; that sort of thing. The game consists of a sequence of screens, each a layer of depth either above or below the last (depending on whether you're ascending or descending in your submarine). In addition to the various items to collect, there are also a few mines floating around that are – as is generally the case with mines – best avoided. In the top screen, water is coloured bright blue, in the next two screens it's coloured dark blue and in the lower three screens everything is black. "How do you avoid mines and detect scrap if the screen is black?" I hear you cry. Cunningly, the submarine has a search light that illuminates four attributes blocks in front of you when activated, turning black water to light cyan. But activating the search light drains the battery of your sub considerably, so it has to be used sparingly. Luckily, there's also an electromagnetic sensor fitted to the submarine that can detect the presence of metal directly below you.

Depth is not – by any stretch of the imagination – a good game, but it would probably have fitted perfectly well on the original Cassette 50, the essence of which could probably be summarized as 'rubbish games that nonetheless take themselves seriously'. And it was lots of fun to write. The problem I encountered was that, when running in BASIC, the redraw of the submarine as it moved – especially when the light was turned on – was so slow as to render the game unplayable. Even by Cassette 50 standards, that's bad. I realized things had to be sped up and used a BASIC compiler – HiSoft's – to achieve this. But we'll come to that in a moment.

Depth was written entirely using *BASin*. The main window is shown below in Figure 5.7. This shows a segment of the program listing with a single line highlighted: in fact, this screenshot was created whilst the game was running (output is given in a separate window that acts more or less as an emulator window) using the *Trace Execution* option available from the *Run* menu. Enabling this slows program execution to a crawl, but highlights the line currently being processed and is an extremely useful way of tracking whether your program is being followed in the manner you intended it to be. *Trace Execution* can be turned on and off at will whilst your program is running, so you don't have to run it from the start at this reduced speed and wait half an hour for it to get to the part you want to examine.

Fig 5.7 BASin's main listing window, with 'Trace Execution' running.

Simply being able to write in BASIC and have instructions parsed – but without the limitations of doing so in an emulator or real Spectrum – is enormously advantageous and time saving. *BASin* comes with a number of additional tools, however, that make the process even more straightforward. These include:

- A renumber facility (available from the Tools menu). This is massively handy for all those insertions you've made between existing lines of code where you need to create more space for additional lines. A danger of some of the renumbering programs that used to be available for the Spectrum was that procedures defined at the end of the program (say at line 8000 onwards) could get dragged forward to the current end of your main program code, but when you select this option, *BASin* asks you if you want to renumber the entire program and – if not – which range of lines you want to renumber. You can also choose the size of the line increments.

- A very comprehensive help system that includes the entire original Sinclair BASIC programming manual.

- A sprite/UDG (User Defined Graphics) tool, also accessed from the *Tools* menu. This very powerful tool enables you to create your 21 UDGs and then send the data statements required to create them straight to your program listing. The method for doing this is a little more complicated than it used to be (the help page for this window, in fact, is a little out of date and describes the old menu options). In the Graphic/Sprite Editor's File menu, select *Export*. Click on the button next to the word 'Memory' under *Import As* and select *Data Decimal*. In the *Import options* area of the panel you now need to specify how many bytes you want per DATA statement line (multiples of eight are tidiest) plus the start line for the first DATA statement and how much to increment line numbers for subsequent statements.

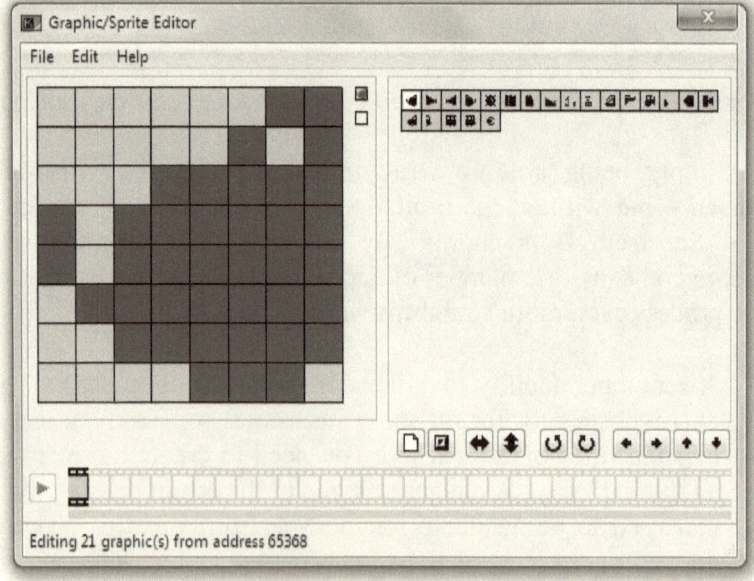

Fig 5.8 BASin's UDG editor

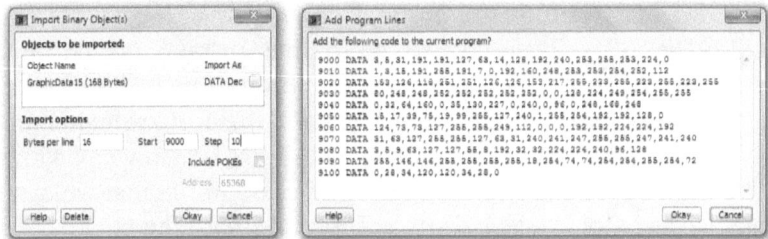

Fig 5.9 The Graphic/Sprite export options panel with the code generated.

Click on Okay and a panel containing your code will appear for your final approval. Click Okay again and into the program listing it goes. You'll still need to write the few lines of code to READ in the data, but a large part of the work has now been done.

- A number of debug windows to help you keep track of what's going on in your program whilst it executes. The variables window, for example, lists the current state of any variables you've defined within your listing.

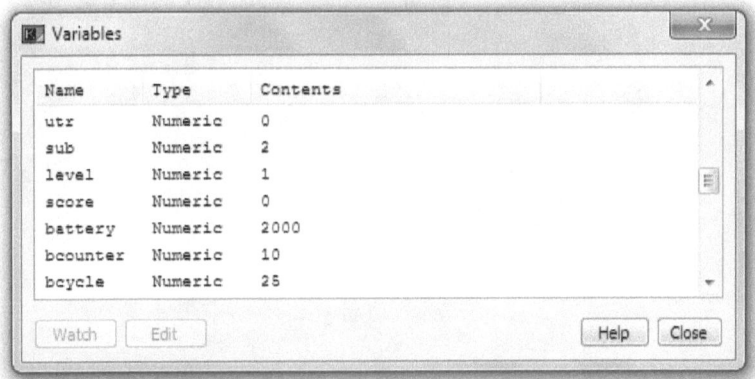

Fig 5.10 BASin's Variables window.

This is by no means an exhaustive list of *BASin's* features, but I don't want to replicate the help file here. The next thing to do is to compile the BASIC listing into machine code. As I mentioned earlier, I'm going to use HiSoft's BASIC compiler, available from *www.worldofspectrum.org/infoseek.cgi?regexp=^HiSoft+BASIC$&pub=^HiSoft$*. There's also an online manual created by the original author of the compiler, Cameron Hayne, which can be accessed at *http://hayne.net/Spectrum/HiSoftBASIC/manual.html*.

We can't do the compiling from within *BASin*, so we need first to save our BASIC program out of it as a cassette file that we can load into an emulator. Select *Tools > Tape Creator*, then click on *Add* in the panel that appears and select *From Current > Program*. Now go to the panel's *File* menu and select *Save Image As*. Enter a name for your file (don't forget to give it a .tap or .tzx extension) then select a location for your tape file and hit Save.

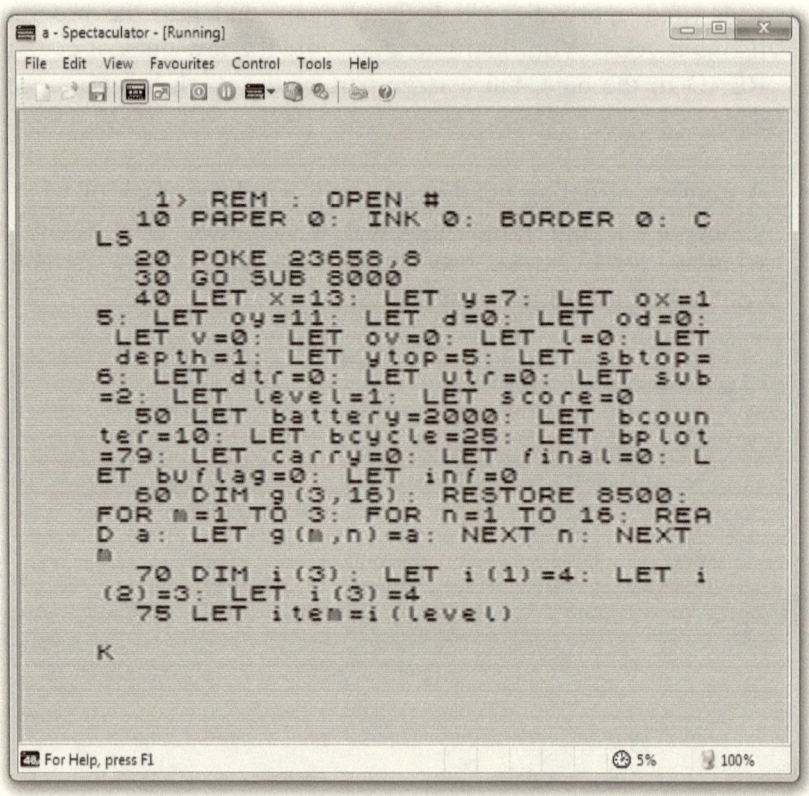

Fig 5.11 The Depth program listing loaded into HiSoft BASIC Compiler. The new line tells it where to start compiling.

Now open up your emulator of choice – I'm going to use *Spectaculator* – and load in HiSoft BASIC. Once it's loaded, you should see the message 'HISOFT BASIC ©1986 Cameron Hayne' across the top of the screen and the usual cursor at the bottom. Change tapes to the cassette you just created and load it in the usual way (ie, without resetting your Spectrum). Hit enter once the load is complete and you should see your listing.

HiSoft BASIC Compiler needs to know where to start compiling, which you can indicate by inserting the statement 'REM: OPEN #' at the very start of the program, as per line 1 in Figure 5.11 above.

I'm not going to go into the finer details of the various compiling options and issues – the manual is perfectly good for that. Suffice to say that the instructions required for *Depth* – because it's quite a long program and contains a lot of DATA statements – are a little more complicated than the usual single '*C' command. Instead, the program has to be compiled in two parts, making sure that RAMTOP is reset between each pass. The sequence required, then is:

```
*X          [Reset RAMTOP]
*D          [Compile DATA statements]
SAVE code
*X          [Reset RAMTOP again]
*E          [Compile rest of program]
SAVE code
```

By contrast, for smaller programs, the usual sequence would be:

```
*C
SAVE code
```

Before saving anything, you need to create a new cassette file to SAVE to. *File > New > Audio cassette file (.tzx)* in Spectaculator. Call this tape, "machine code". Once the compiler has completed each of its passes, it tells you the exact instruction you need to type in to save the machine code, plus the exact instruction you need to load it in back later. It's important to make a note of the latter before saving – you'll need that later when you come to create your BASIC loader. The first of my two screens giving this information – complete with my SAVE command typed in (just waiting for the Enter key to be pressed) is shown in Figure 5.12 below. Make sure you remember to press the record button on the tape browser panel before hitting Enter on your SAVE command.

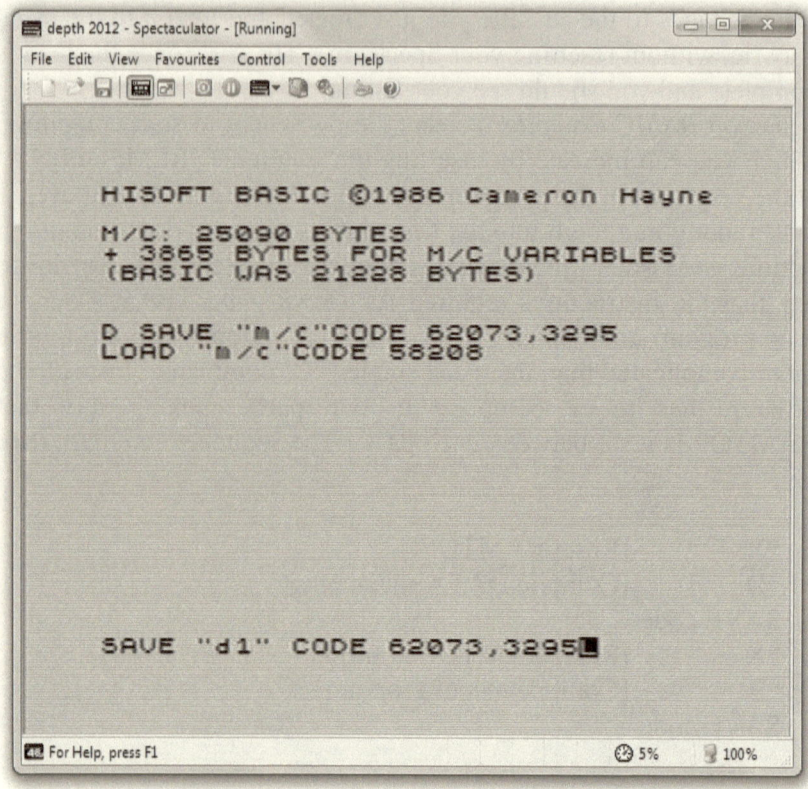

Fig 5.12 The feedback screen at the end of a compile.

So now we have saved to cassette our machine code program. We just need to create a BASIC loader that will load it in and – for, what Spectrum game would be complete without one? – a loading screen. For Depth's loading screen I used *ZX-Paintbrush* by Claus Jahn, which I chose because it allowed me to use windows fonts for a great-looking title (in fact *BASin* now also has a screen editor that supports windows fonts, so you could return to this if you prefer not to learn another application) plus it has a great selection of drawing tools.

Once you've created your loading screen, you need to save it out as another .TZX file. Select *File* > *Save As* and select the file type 'Complex tape files (*.tzx)' from the drop down list. Call this tape, "loading screen" and give the header itself a name like 'ls'.

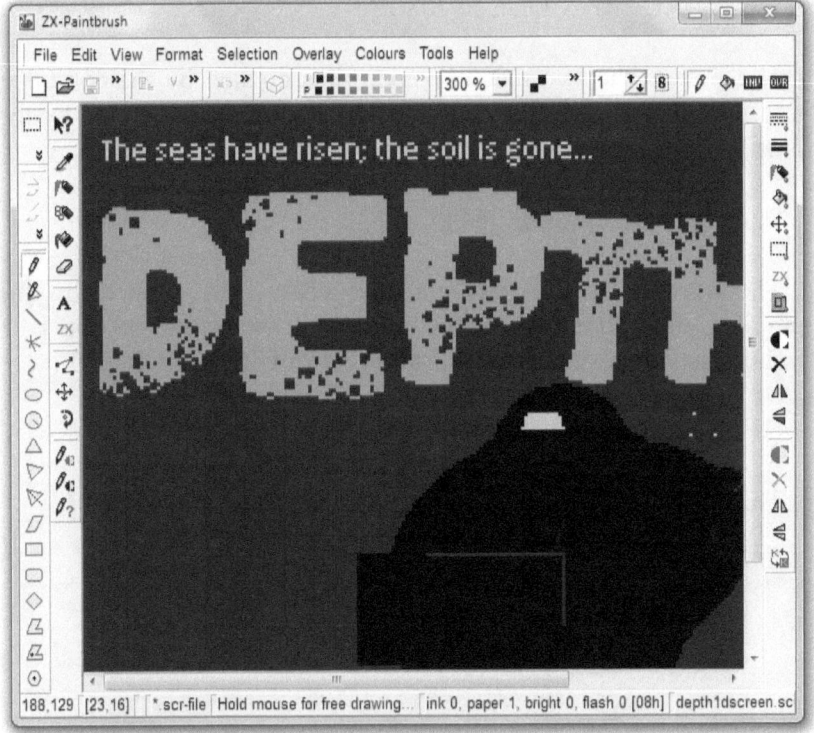

Fig 5.13 The loading screen is prepared in ZX-Paintbrush.

And now we need to create the BASIC loader. Reset your Spectrum in *Spectaculator* and create a new – ie, a third – cassette file. Call this one 'loader'. Here's the listing for mine.

10   BORDER 1: PAPER 1: INK 1: CLS

This turns the screen dark blue and clears it.

20   CLEAR 36444

36444 is the memory address where the machine code will load; we need to make sure it's clear and this line performs that function.

30   LOAD "" SCREEN$

This will load the loading screen.

    40   LOAD "d1" CODE 58208

The first of the two machine code files created by the compiler. Note how I'm loading the code into the address given to me by the compiler (see Figure 5.12).

    50 LOAD "e1" CODE 36445

The second of the two machine code files created by the compiler; the address 36445 was given to me on the second pass (and this is why I've cleared the address from 36444 in line 20).

    60 RANDOMIZE USR 36445

This will run the machine code.

Fig 5.14 The complete BASIC loader ready to be saved.

When you save the file to tape, don't forget to add 'LINE 10' to the end of the SAVE instruction (as per Figure 5.14) so that the program runs automatically when it loads.

We now have three separate tape files: 'loader', 'loading screen' and 'machine code'. Our last task is to put these together onto one tape. To do this, we'll use Claus Jahn's *ZX-Blockeditor*. First of all, open it with the first of these cassette files (ie, 'loader.tzx'). *File* menu > *Open* and locate your file.

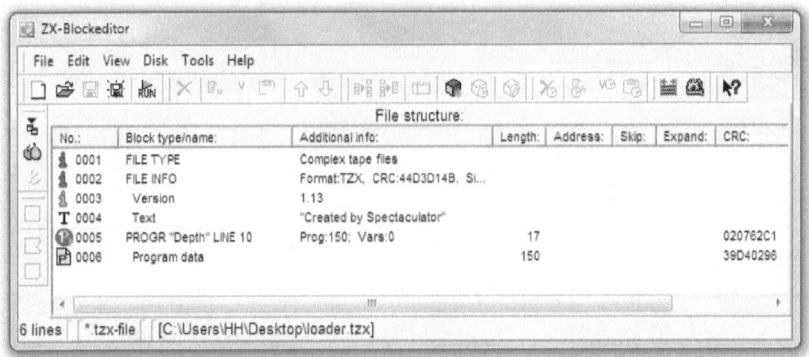

Fig 5.15 ZX-Blockeditor displaying the BASIC loader.

You should now see something similar to the panel shown in Figure 5.15. Notice the meta information displayed, such as what program the .TZX file was created with and what line it will run from. *ZX-Blockeditor* comes with a whole range of tools and features, including tools to manipulate disk files as well as cassette files. The range of file formats that the application supports, in fact, is quite staggering. But I'll leave you to explore all of these at your leisure. Our task now is to add the next bit of the tape we're creating: the loading screen. To do this, select *Tools > Import file* and locate the next cassette file (ie, 'loading screen.tzx'). The block information from the 'loading screen.tzx' file should now be added to the list of block information in the main window. It's as simple as that.

Repeat this step with the 'machine code.tzx' cassette file and your *ZX-Blockeditor* main window should look pretty much like the panel in Figure 5.16. That's it: our virtual cassette is done. All that remains is to save it: Select *File > Save as* and give your cassette creation a name. Now load it into your favourite emulator and

76 The ZX Spectrum on your PC

enjoy.

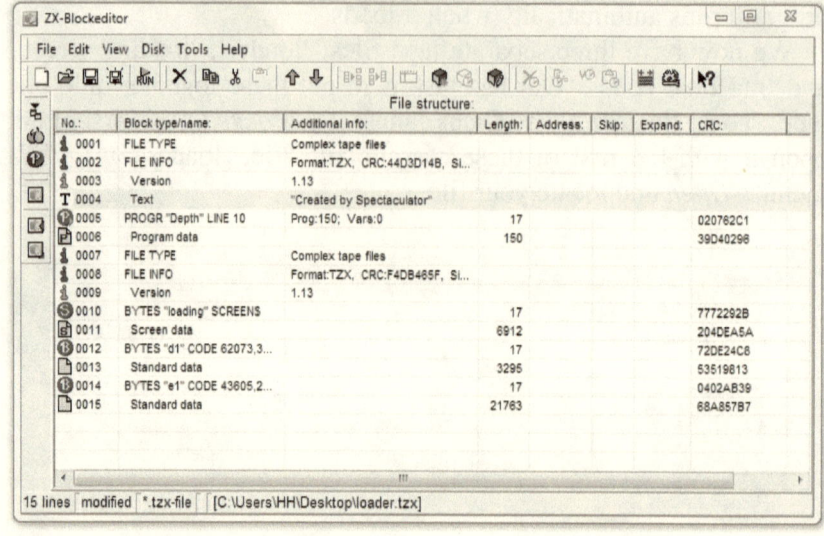

Fig 5.16 ZX-Blockeditor displaying the final tape file contents.

Chapter Six
Spectrum clones

If imitation is the sincerest form of flattery then the Spectrum has plenty to blush about. It's been estimated there could easily have been as many as 100 different unofficial versions of the Spectrum made worldwide (it's been suggested there were 50 in Russia alone).

Of course there were the official versions also. These were the result of Sinclair's various partnerships with other companies, such as *Timex* in America and *Investronica* in Spain. It was with Investronica, for example, that the Spectrum 128 was developed, going on sale in Spain almost half a year before it was launched in the UK (Sinclair had a whole pile of Spectrum pluses it wanted to get rid of over the Christmas period before launching it).

The *Timex Sinclair* partnership was *Sinclair's* way of getting into the US market and resulted in the *TS* range of computers - the TS1000 and TS1500 being American versions of the ZX81 and the TS2068 being the American version of the ZX Spectrum. In fact the TS2068 was quite an improvement on the British Spectrum, sporting built-in joystick ports, a cartridge port, three channel sound via an AY sound chip and - most impressive of all - extra video modes: one doubled the Spectrum's horizontal screen resolution, making it much more suitable for word processing; another reduced attribute clash massively by enabling two colours per character *line* of eight pixels rather than just two per eight by eight character (ie, up to 16 colours could be displayed per character). The TS2068 was released in late 1983, which of course begs the question: why weren't either of these video modes built-in to the Spectrum 128 in 1986? The TS2068 was only compatible with about 10% of Spectrum software, however (a Spectrum emulator cartridge had to be plugged in to get 100% compatibility); it's been speculated this might well have been one of the reasons for its downfall, for the

TS2068 was nothing like as successful as its British counterpart and was withdrawn from sale in 1984.

Meanwhile *Timex Portugal* released its own version of the computer - The *TC2068* - for European use (compatible with European televisions and with a Spectrum-style edge connector where the TS2068 had used a ZX81-style connector) and a 'cut down' version without the cartridge port and AY chip called the *TC2048*. This latter version was actually almost 100% compatible with Spectrum software. Although it didn't have the AY sound chip it *did* retain the video modes of the *TS* and *TC2068*. Very little software was produced for it, however, which is a great shame.

Ironically, the *un*offical clones also often ended up more advanced than the original hardware we were stuck with in the UK. Our Soviet friends, for example, to whom we refused to sell the machines to (because they might use them to launch a nuclear attack on us, presumably) became quite adept at smuggling Spectrums back home to the motherland. I used to wonder what it was about the Spectrum that had appealed so much to the Eastern Europeans; apparently (I read this once and can't remember where) it was just that it was small enough to stick down your jumper. Fair enough, if it's true; imagine trying to smuggle out a Commodore 64 that way.

Once Spectrums were across the Iron Curtain, they got reverse engineered by hobbyists so that equivalent machines could be put together using the parts and components available locally. Amongst the many local variations, a few machines became notable, the most famous of which is undoubtedly the Russian *Pentagon*. The Pentagon wasn't a computer you bought in a shop, it was a design circulated amongst enthusiasts that you put together yourself. For this reason, no two Pentagons are likely to look the same, since the casing would be up to you and dependent on what you had available. But a fairly 'standard' approach now has become to mount the motherboard inside a PC-type case and connect a separate keyboard and monitor.

But here's the deal - the Russians didn't stop with just reverse engineering the Spectrum, oh no; and here we see the benefits of allowing technology to 'evolve' in this way. In addition to adopting the Spectrum as their preferred platform, they also adopted a disk interface as 'standard' - the BETA disk interface developed for the Spectrum by UK firm *Technology Research Ltd*, with its TR-DOS operating system. Quite why it was this system which should be chosen - which made pretty much no impact whatsoever in the UK market it was intended for - instead of more popular formats over here such as the MGT Disciple/Plus D format is probably a question which will never be answered. Nonetheless, whilst we were all still faithfully loading software into our machines via cassette, the disk drive had become in the Soviet Union a standard storage medium for Spectrum software. In the manner that is so often identified as a key characteristic of eastern European societies (and also, incidentally, of the Spectrum and its software), restriction and limitation had become the source for ingenuity and innovation.

The importance of the eastern European clones in particular to the longevity of the Spectrum cannot be underestimated. Although we are now enjoying in the UK a bit of a purple patch for new Spectrum software, for many years following the end of the Spectrum's commercial life, releases such as this were extremely thin on the ground. In fact, it was the eastern European scene that pretty much kept Spectrum software alive, in particular through the demo scene, still vibrant in many of these countries today. Take a brief look at the WoS archive and you'll find that there are almost as many TR-DOS disk images listed as there are +3 disk images. Unlike the +3 disks, however, these are not games you can also get hold of on tape or in tape files (many of the +3 releases were actually available also on cassette, so the main advantage of obtaining a version on disk was often just faster loading times). Basically, a whole new dimension to Spectrum computing. And quite a refreshing one too, because the ideas and presentation in these programs are often quite different from that of the western software with which we are familiar. The technical skill with which TR-DOS programs are put together is also often breath-taking. If you want to see a good example of what can be achieved on a Russian machine, get hold of a copy of *Fire and Ice* (see Appendix B) and a Pentagon enabled emulator and be prepared to be blown away.

Support for Russian machines and TR-DOS, therefore, is a key feature of many Spectrum emulators. The two most emulated clones are the *Pentagon* and the *Scorpion,* both of which are supported by *Spectaculator*. *ZX SPIN* supports just the *Pentagon*. The two main TR-DOS file formats that emulators use for TR-DOS disk images are .TRD and .SCL. TRD files are dumps of a whole disk image, empty spaces and all, whilst SCL files are only as big as the actual TR-DOS files they contain (although they still work just the same as TRD images). The capacity of an empty .TRD file is 640K (equating to a double sided, double density 3.5 inch floppy, although in fact the original Beta Disk interface was also designed to be used with a range of other drives, including 3 inch and 5.25 inch), so a .TRD file containing a 10K Spectrum program would still be 640K in size, whilst its .SCL equivalent would be just 10K.

And support for the Timex-Sinclair clones? Somewhat ironically – given that these were actually 'official' Spectrum variants – this is much harder to find in Spectrum emulators. There is no support for the TS range in either *Spectaculator* or *SPIN*. Probably the best emulator to use if you would like to experience the US and Portuguese versions of the Spectrum is Mike Wynne's *EightyOne* (see Chapter Seven for more details of this emulator).

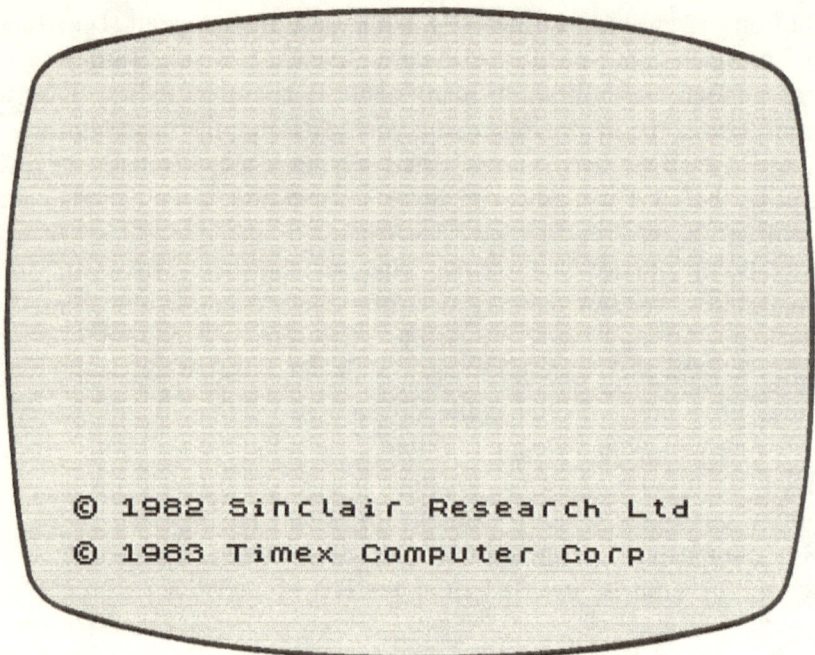

Fig 6.1 The TS2068 boot screen displaying in EightyOne.

Working with TR-DOS

To select Pentagon mode on *Spectaculator,* click the mode selector icon (the little Spectrum picture) and choose *Pentagon 128.* To view the disk drive panel select *View > Disk Drives*. TR-DOS supports up to four disk drives, which you can configure from the *Beta 128* tab on the main *Options* panel (*Tools > Options*). To select a particular disk image, click on the word 'Empty' next to a drive letter and find the image you're after on your hard drive.

To select Pentagon mode on *ZX SPIN*, select *Tools > Options > Hardware* and on the *Spectrum Model* tab select *Pentagon 128*. To view the four disk drives (all attached by default in *SPIN*), select *File > Insert Disks;* click on the little folder icons to load disk images into these drives.

Both the *Pentagon 128* and the *Scorpion 256* employ variants on the 128K Spectrum's menu system. For the *Pentagon,* the layout of the main menu is identical to that of the original 128 except that in the place of the original 'Tape Tester' we now have a TR-DOS option. On the *Scorpion,* there are two TR-DOS options - one for 48k and one for 128K. Generally speaking, you can make the expectation of most TR-DOS software that it will load in the *Pentagon*'s TR-DOS mode (ie, this seems to be the default). Scroll down, hit ENTER and you are now at the main TR-DOS command line.

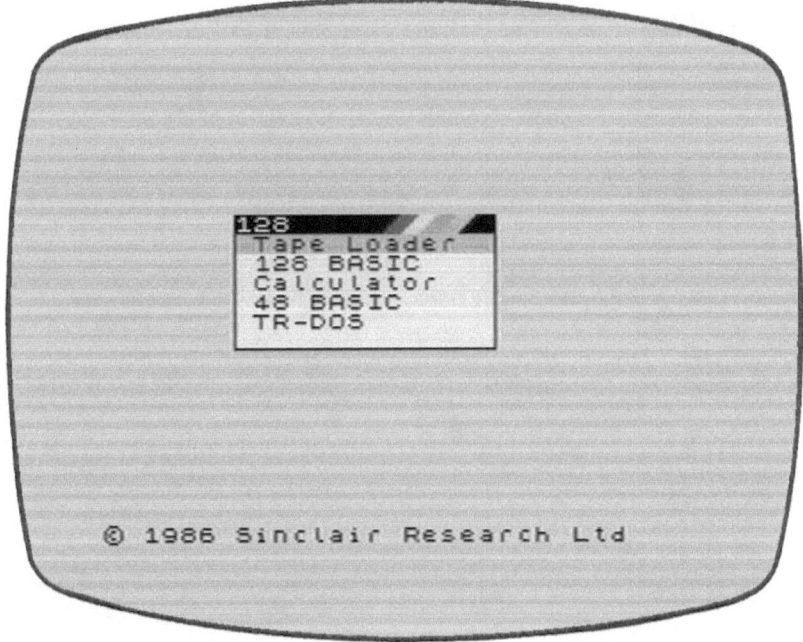

Fig 6.2 The Pentagon main menu.

At the TR-DOS command prompt, *CAT* (*symbol-shift 9* in extended mode) will list your disk's contents. TR-DOS works with drive A as its default; to change drive type *"b:" for drive B, *"c:" for C and *"d:" for D. Your commands after this are the usual LOAD "filename", SAVE "filename", etc that you're used to; an exception is the *RUN* command, which you can use to LOAD and RUN a BASIC program (ie, RUN "game"). To get out of the command prompt and back to the normal Spectrum menu type *RETURN* (just the Y key) and ENTER.

As with all other media on *Spectaculator,* creating a new TR-DOS disk image is simply a matter of selecting *File > New*; select either *Blank TR-DOS disk (.scl)* or *Blank TR-DOS disk (.trd)*. ZX SPIN does not support the creation of new TR-DOS disk images.

Chapter Seven
Other PC emulators

There have been so many Spectrum emulators developed for the PC and other platforms that it would be remiss of me to neglect to mention at least a few others. We've focused so far on *Spectaculator* and *ZX SPIN* because I find these arguably the most comprehensive *and* user-friendly of the Windows emulators about at present (no doubt, many will disagree with me); but that's not to say that other emulators have nothing further to offer. Far from it. There's a wide range of additional features to be found in other emulators.

In this chapter, therefore, we'll take a brief look at some of the other PC emulators and their distinguishing features. I can't cover every single emulator about – that would take a whole book in its own right – and so I apologise in advance for those in the know who feel I've omitted to mention a particular emulator or emulator feature they feel to be important. All of the emulators, unless otherwise stated, are of course available from the *Emulators* page at WoS. I've covered them in alphabetical order to prevent anyone from attempting to read any hierarchical significance into my order of presentation (the scene – like any other – is not without its politics) plus I've covered a number of quite old emulators (because of their historical significance) which might not be the best applications to jump into for Windows emulation (but which might be perfect if you have an old laptop lying around that you would like to turn into a dedicated Spectrum emulator).

A final point before we get going. This book is called 'The ZX Spectrum on Your PC' and it's generally assumed by this that the PC in question is running Microsoft Windows. I won't be covering Linux emulators (also available from the *Emulators* page at WoS) for two key reasons. Firstly, I don't have a Linux PC (ok, I did once have an EeePC running Linux, but I never got on with it when it came to installing new software on it; it was like rubbing my face in broken glass and – yes – I know that's because I'm stupid) and therefore cannot talk from experience. Secondly, if you're IT-savvy enough to be running a Linux system, you almost certainly don't need the likes of me to be talking you through the basics of Spectrum emulation. I salute you, Linux people: please don't be offended by this omission. The same goes for Macs, by the way (but with a bit less love and adoration).

EightyOne by Mike Wynne

EightyOne is one of the more recent additions to the Spectrum emulator scene. As its name suggests, it started out life as a Sinclair ZX81 emulator and grew (and grew and grew) from there. To the best of my knowledge, it's the emulator that supports the widest range of Z80 hardware; at the time of writing, this is the ZX80, the ZX81, the 16K Spectrum, the 48K Spectrum, the original 128K Spectrum, the Spectrum +2, +3 and +2A, the Sinclair QL, the Timex-Sinclair TS1000 and TS1500 (US versions of the ZX81), the Timex-Sinclair TS2068, the Timex-Portugal TC2048, the Lambda 8300 (a ZX81 clone from Lambda Electronics Limited), the Ringo R470 (a Brazilian clone of the ZX81 by Ritas do Brasil), the TK85 (another Brazilian ZX81 clone by Microdigital Eletronica) and the Jupiter Ace (a Z80 micro by ex-Sinclair designers Richard Altwasser and Steven Vickers that was distinctive for using FORTH instead of BASIC). It also supports homebrew projects the ZX97 Lite and the ZX Spectrum SE. A large range of peripherals are also covered. My particular favourite of these is the ZX81 RAM pack (which expanded the ZX81's memory from 1K to 16K). Of course, the RAM pack being a Sinclair add-on peripheral meant that it was notorious for crashing the computer if it was ever moved (for example, if you pulled the computer slightly towards you), a phenomena that became affectionately known (not so affectionately at the time, of course) as RAM pack wobble. You'll be pleased to hear that *EightyOne* includes RAM pack wobble emulation. Yes.

As mentioned in Chapter Three, EightyOne is also my favourite emulator for TV display emulation. Features include ghosting, dot crawl, brightness and contrasts controls, and picture roll.

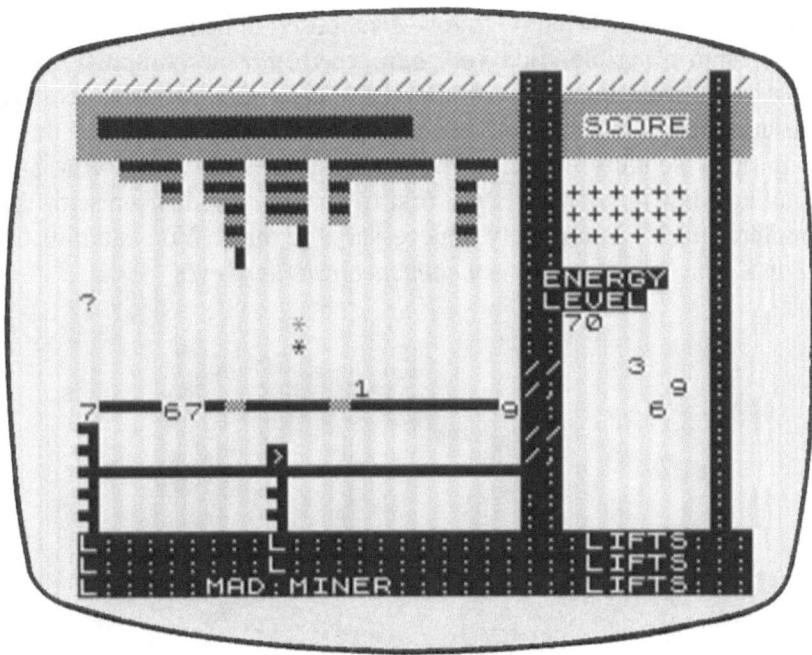

Fig 7.1 A ZX81 game running in EightyOne.

EmuZWin by Vladimir Kladov

Vladimir Kladov's *EmuZWin* has made its mark through its support for 256 colour games, a format first developed by *Iñigo Ayo* and *David Goti* for their own emulator Spec256. *Spec256* hasn't been developed for over a decade now, due in part to the lack of interest in developing new 256 colour overlays (the idea is to take an existing game snapshot and then map onto it a 256 colour 'overlay' which is then substituted in for the game's original colours). *EmuZWin's* in-built 256 colour overlay editor makes creating new overlays much more straightforward, however. A dedicated web page for 256 coloured in Spectrum games has been published at *www.yantragames.com/ZX256.html.*

256 colour games is only one of *EmuZWin*'s features, of course; it also features an in-built map editor and a rather nifty menu link to an external program called *Lens Key* written by *Simon Owen*. *Lens Key* is a tiny utility that decodes the optical scrambling of *Lenslok* protected games such as *Tomahawk* and *Elite*. The *Lenslok* itself

was a little plastic window that was supposed to bend the jumble on screen into a legible code you then typed into the computer. Oh, what fun I used to have with *Lenslok*. *Lens Key* performs exactly the same function as this device except – in contrast to the real thing – it does actually work. The application will work with any emulator, but *EmuZWin* is the first to actually call it from with the emulator itself. Completely unnecessary, but nice. You can pick up *Lens Key* at *http://simonowen.com/spectrum/lenskey/*.

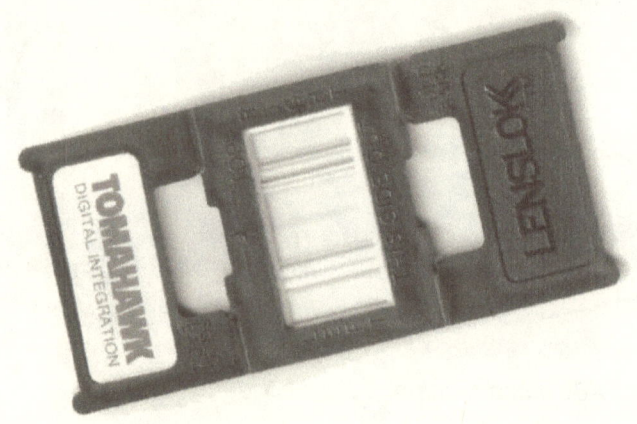

Fig 7.2 Good old Lenslock.

Es.pectrum by Javier Chocano

Any complete discussion of official Spectrum variants (as opposed to the Russian and Eastern European clones), should make mention also of the Spanish machines. Just as Sinclair joint-ventured in the US with Timex, so it teamed up with *Investronica* in Spain. It was actually *Investronica* who developed the first Spectrum 128, which was released in Spain in 1985 - the British version wasn't released until the following year.

The Spanish 128 is pretty much identical, hardware-wise, to the British version, however it didn't use the familiar menu system of the British 128 - that was developed later. Instead it features a built-in text editor; it's not particularly complex and greatly inferior to the various word processors of the day (which is probably why Sinclair dropped it for the British version in favour of a more user-friendly interface); but it's a curiosity, nonetheless. Which brings us nicely to Spanish Spectrum emulator *Es.pectrum* by *Javier Chocano*. In addition to all the British machines and the Russian *Pentagon* and *Scorpion* clones, *Es.pectrum* also emulates all the Spanish variants on the Spectrum also. A French version of the +2 is included too for good measure. It's certainly one of the biggest range of official models I've seen an emulator cover.

Fuse by Philip Kendall et al.

Fuse – the Free Unix Spectrum Emulator – is one of the pioneers of Spectrum emulation, particularly where new hardware developments are concerned. If there's a new hardware project in progress and only one emulator supports it, you can be reasonably certain that this will be Fuse. Fuse currently supports the ZXATASP interface, the ZXCF interface (both mass storage devices by Sami Vehmaa) and the DivIDE interface. A patch is available for ULAplus support and I understand an uncompiled version is available giving support for Spectranet (for both of these projects, see Chapter Eight). Fuse is also one of the very few Spectrum emulators to support the Opus Discovery disk drive system.

In addition to these cutting edge features, Fuse emulates all British Spectrums, all the Timex Spectrums, the Pentagon and Scorpion, and the Spectrum +3e and ZX Spectrum SE homebrew clones. It includes support for the MGT +D, the Interface 1, the Interface 2 and TR-DOS. It comes with .RZX support, a built-in debugger and memory browser, and a nice little menu of filters that can be applied to the display (my favourite being 'Dot-Matrix', which looks uncannily like my old Fergusson TV).

Fuse is an emulator for Linux, however there is a Windows port available from the WoS emulators page, which is what I use. I find the menus on this a little hard to navigate, which is probably an artefact of being written for a different operating system and different expectations. To make the emulator window bigger on screen, for example, you have to click on the lower-right corner of window, hold your mouse button down and stretch until you reach the doubled size (nothing will happen until that point). There's no menu option that I can find to do this and it took me an *age* to work it out. But Fuse is definitely worth persevering with. To many Spectrum old-timers, it's the connoisseur's choice of emulator. It's also free, so it's not like you have anything to lose.

RealSpectrum by Ramsoft

For a long time, *Ramsoft*'s *RealSpectrum* – a DOS emulator – was the Spectrum emulator that stood head and shoulders above the rest. It is still an extremely comprehensive emulator and it continues to offer features that other emulators don't. It is also well worth a look if you're planning on setting up a Spectrum emulator on an older machine, especially if it's a machine with a 3.5 inch floppy drive.

RealSpectrum comes in two versions - the main DOS build (*RSDOS*) for MSDOS and Windows up to 98, and a version that will run on Windows XP (*RS32*). One of the key features of this emulator was its support for a very wide range of disk interfaces, including the *Beta 128* disk interface discussed in the last chapter, *MGT*'s *Disciple* and *Plus D* interfaces and the *Opus Discovery* interface and drive. Of particular importance so far as these devices were concerned was *RealSpectrum's* 'RealDisk' support for many of them, allowing you to access or create actual floppy disks for these systems via your PC's floppy disk drive, if you had one (although this doesn't work for *RS32*). If you once used any of these disk interfaces and still have the floppies in a box in the attic, therefore, *RealSpectrum* might well be your solution for retrieving the files from them you thought you might never see again. RealSpectrum also supported some of the 'homebrew' hardware developments in the DIY hardware scene such as Garry Lancaster's *+3e* hard disk Interface and ROMs and Sami Vehmaa's *ZXCF* compact flash interface.

RealSpectrum is not available from the WoS emulators page, the link having been removed at *Ramsoft's* request. I recall a falling out between *Ramsoft* and a number of people in the Spectrum community (I can't remember the details), which was a big shame because – at the time – *Ramsoft* were reportedly working on the next-big-thing in PC emulation, a Windows emulator code-named *RealX*. In the event, *Ramsoft* withdrew from the emulation scene and nothing more was heard of this project. Happily, however, *RealSpectrum* – in all its various forms – is still available from its old site at *http://ramsoft.bbk.org.omegahg.com/realspec.html*. My understanding is that this page disappeared for a while, so if you don't have any luck with this link, a mirror is available at *http://zxm.speccy.cz/realspec/*.

Fig 7.3 Sami Vehmaa's ZXCF compact flash interface – attached here to a rubber-keyed Spectrum via an IF 1 – is emulated by Fuse.

Speccy by Marat Fayzullin

Speccy is written in C, making it portable, the author asserts, to other platforms. The significance of this is that there is also a version of this emulator for Android devices (see Chapter Nine). As a Windows emulator, Speccy emulates a fine range of models – all the British Spectrums, the Didaktik Gama (a Slovak Spectrum clone) the Pentagon, the Scorpion, the Timex-Sinclair TS2068 and the Timex Portugal TC2048. It supports the Kempston and AMX mouse and a number of peripherals, including the Disciple/+D, the Interface 1 and the ZX Printer. It also has a rather nifty little feature that allows you to play AY music through your PC's MIDI wavetable – which worked a lot better than I thought it would.

Despite these fine features, I had a few issues with this emulator. To start with, the screen flickers a great deal on my computer – and I don't think this is a design feature. Secondly, the Spectrum border isn't emulated (I can't think why this would be omitted in a PC emulator, where there's plenty of space for it). Thirdly, there seems to be no option to flashload tape files, meaning you have to wait for tapes to load in (whether you're in a nostalgic mood or not). As always, I worry with such criticism that I simply haven't looked hard enough to find out how to do something, but my rule of thumb is that if I can't find it after five minutes of searching through various menus then it's either not there or not enough thought has been put in to the user-interface.

SpecEmu by Mark Woodmass

SpecEmu, by *SPIN* co-author *Mark Woodmass,* is an intriguing little emulator with a quite eclectic mix of features. On the one hand a good working emulator that supports all the British models (and the Pentagon and the Timex TC2048), *SpecEmu* has about it also the slight sense of a mad scientist's laboratory. I think the reason I feel this way about it is due to the absence of features I'm expecting to find in an emulator this complex (such as Interface 1 and ZX Printer emulation) whilst at the same time emulating hardware that can't be found anywhere else (such as the *Currah μsource* plug-in assembler/debugger, which I hadn't even heard of before seeing the little tick box for it here, perhaps because Currah went into liquidation before it was ever released). *SpecEmu* also emulates the *DivIDE* hard disk interface (see Chapter Eight). One gets the feeling that this is an emulator that Mark has written for himself, and this personality endears it very much to me.

Also an emulator with a sense of humour, *SpecEmu* includes an option to simulate the infamous audio distortion of the Spectrum +3! Although TV display emulation is not as authentic as *Spectaculator* or *EightyOne*, 'ULA colour ramping' introduces a satisfactory ghosting to pixels and the very daft and yet somehow glorious 'enable extremely dodgy television set' periodically interrupts the display and sound with bursts of white noise.

A slightly newer version of *SpecEmu* than the one available from WoS also supports the *ULAplus* (again, see Chapter Eight) and Andrew Owen's *SE BASIC*. This is available from the ULAplus website: *http://sites.google.com/site/ulaplus/*

Spud by Richard Chandler

Spud is an emulator under current development and currently supports only the British Spectrum models (ie, the Sinclair 16K, 48K and 128K models; the Amstrad +2, +3 and +2A). It doesn't support any peripherals at the moment, however it does offer some support for ULAplus (see Chapter Eight). It works with all variants of snapshot file and can load from (but not save to) .TZX files. It also has quite brilliant tape wobble emulation.

What makes *Spud* stand out (other than its brilliant tape wobble emulation) is its comprehensive debug menu, offering a whole range of views on the machine's current state. It also has a sprite search tool and a handy logic calculator, making this very much an emulator for developers. Nice.

UnrealSpeccy by deathsoft

UnrealSpeccy, originally by SMT, then taken on by Alone Coder and now maintained by deathsoft, is a hugely influential Russian Spectrum emulator supporting a number of Eastern European clones and add-on hardware. The executable in the current download from WoS attempts and then fails to compile this emulator. I'm not sure what I'm doing wrong and can't find any instructions to guide me. *UnrealSpeccy* has been ported to a number of different platforms, however – including Android – so can be experienced there.

vbSpec by Miklos Muhi

VbSpec, initially a creation of Chris Cowley but then taken on by Miklos Muhi, is a Spectrum emulator written entirely in Visual BASIC. Which is impressive. By current standards, it's a little basic (no pun intended) in terms of its features, but it is still one of the few Spectrum emulators to support the *Timex TC2048*. And its ZX Printer has a form feed button. It's the little things that count.

Warajevo by Samir Ribic and Zeljko Juric

No longer maintained and a DOS emulator for much older PCs than the current standard, *Warajevo* is nonetheless a highly significant Spectrum emulator. Developed in Sarajevo during the Bosnian War by *Samir Ribic* and *Zeljko Juric*, the emulator was an attempt by these two "to remove the dark thoughts" from their heads. Amidst falling grenades, sniper fire, power-cuts and very little food to eat, *Warajevo* was a lifeline to its developers because it reminded them "of all of the times when, in [their] neighbour-hoods, the life was nice and normal". It was one of the first Spectrum emulators for the PC and you can read the fascinating story of its development here: *www.worldofspectrum.org/warajevo/Story.html*

X128 by James McKay

X128 is a DOS Spectrum emulator written by *James McKay* that supports a wide range of file types, including .TRD TR-DOS disk images and .MGT *Disciple* disk images. Like most DOS emulators, it's not happy on Windows XP and above, but on earlier versions of Windows it works just fine. Speaking personally, this is the emulator that seems to work for me on overstretched systems when others fail. I have a very old Toshiba laptop that just about runs Windows 98 on 16Mb RAM, for example, and *X128* seems quite at home there.

Zero by Arjun Nair

Zero is a Spectrum emulator under current development, and very fancy looking it is too. Coming in a shiny black skin that resembles the Spectrum's original aesthetics, the emulator also sports one of the best looking tape browsers I've seen so far. This not only gives the standard information on tape file blocks, it also displays meta information on the title loaded. It also – and this is my favourite bit (by now, you must be getting a feel for the sad sort of thing that excites me) renders a photo of a C60 cassette with the title of your tape file written on it. Genius. The emulator offers built-in searching of and downloading from WoS, though doesn't then do the last little bit and actually load that file into the cassette deck (ie, you have to save it to your hard disk then open it using the tape browser). All cassette formats are supported for loading, but not for saving.

Zero offers fairly limited hardware support, offering only the Sinclair 48K and 128K spectrums (there is also the 128Ke, which I understand to be an 'ideal Spectrum' with all the bugs sorted out) and no peripheral emulation. There is, however, some support for ULAplus (see Chapter Eight). There's also a comprehensive debugger.

Like Fuse, I couldn't work out how to resize the window on *Zero*. I can't believe this is impossible – since it makes for a rather tiny emulator – but, in the end, I gave up trying. To run *Zero,* you'll need the SlimDX and .Net Framework. If you don't have these installed on your PC, download the setup installation from *www.yantragames.com/Zero%20Setup.exe* (rather than the zip file from the WoS emulators page) and this will take care of that for you.

ZX32 by Vaggelis Kapartzianis

ZX32 was one of the first Windows emulators and stood its ground for a long time as a very popular, very widely used program. It hasn't actually been updated since 2000 and, as such, does not compare well on features next to the likes of *SPIN* and *Spectaculator*.

Z80 by Gerton Lunter

I can't not mention *Z80*, one of the very first Spectrum emulators, dating back to 1991 (pre-dating even Warajevo). This was my first ever PC emulator of any description and I ran it on my black and white Amstrad 286. In its day, *Z80* was shareware, but Gerton has now removed this restriction and you can download the full Windows version – *WinZ80* – from WoS (but, sadly, not the DOS full version, with its instructions for building a parallel printer cassette interface; you can though still download the shareware DOS version and this will work under Windows 7 using the *DOSBOX* DOS emulator). *WinZ80* will not work with Windows 7, so you'll need an older computer and operating system to run it on – ideally a Windows 95 system. The emulator was last updated in 1999.

Chapter Eight
Emulating homebrew hardware

In addition to all the 'officially released' peripherals back in the Spectrum's day, there have also been plenty of 'homebrew' hardware projects developed for the machine in more recent years. Mass storage on a hard disk or flash media card has been a particular area of interest. Of course, home-made hardware generally isn't available to buy online, since producing and distributing it in large numbers would be very time-consuming and difficult to do at a reasonable cost; rather, the schematics are made available so that electronics hobbyists can create them for themselves. Occasionally, however, batches of hardware do get made up and sold. The two main suppliers I'm aware of can be found at *www.rwapsoftware.co.uk/spectrum.html* and *www.sintechshop.de/en/sinclair*.

It's certainly well beyond the remit of this book as a beginners' guide to go into these projects in detail, but it's worth spending a little time at least on a few of the more prolific projects, particularly since they are emulated by some of the Spectrum emulators (you might like at this point to keep a finger in the previous chapter) if you want to find out more about some of the emulators mentioned here), enabling you to see what they would look like if ever the temptation did come your way to try hardware upgrades for real.

Storage

Perhaps the most high-profile of the storage devices is the *DivIDE* project. An interface for what at the time of its inception (the mid-noughties) was the standard type of PC hard disk connection (Parallel ATA (IDE) – or PATA – as opposed to Serial ATA – or SATA – which is the standard type fitted to most PCs these days),

DivIDE has been through a number of different versions and has been highly desired peripheral for members of the Spectrum community still using original hardware, such as demo-scene coders (who require such precision access to Spectrum timings that the real thing is frequently preferable to an emulator). There are also a number of enthusiasts who enjoy such challenges as mounting an original Spectrum motherboard inside a PC case and attaching all manner of modern glitter (as a random example, see *bverstee's* project at *www.youtube.com/watch?v=LvWjezDrwdY*; in fact, this uses the *MB02* IDE hard disk interface rather than the *DivIDE*, which is emulated by *RealSpectrum*).

DivIDE is supported by a number of emulators, including *EightyOne, Fuse, SpecEmu* and *ZX SPIN*. To use the interface on these programs, you'll need a formatted hard disk image, the standard for which is the .HDF file format (originally created by *Ramsoft*). Creating .HDF files from scratch is a pretty complicated process; you need to first of all create a drive on a removable device such as an SD card, then convert this drive to an .HDF file using *Drive image & ZX file transfer.*

1. Format an SD or compact flash card (something no more than 2GB) to FAT16. To do this, you'll need to open up a Command window. For Windows XP, click on Start menu > select Run and type 'CMD' in the box then press return; for Windows 7, click on the Windows button, type 'CMD' in the 'Search programs and files' box and hit return.

2. Once you're into the command window, type 'Format H: /FS:FAT' where H is the drive letter of the card you want to use as your DivIDE hard disk. *Double check this!* If one of your PC's regular drives is labelled H you will destroy all data on it.

3. Close the command window.

4. Copy some Spectrum games onto your newly formatted card in the way you would normally copy and paste files (eg, using Windows Explorer). Accepted formats are .Z80 and .SNA snapshot files, .TAP tape files and .SCR screen files.

5. Download the *Drive image & ZX file transfer* utility

(*http://velesoft.speccy.cz/zx/divide/software/drive_image_&_zx_file_transfer-by_putnik.zip*) and use it to make a hard disk file (HDF) image of your SD card.

6. The emulator I've found to be most reliable with *DivIDE* is *SpecEmu* by Mark Woodmass. To configure it, select *Options > Options > Hardware* and tick the DivIDE box. There are a number of different firmware operating systems for use with the DivIDE, which you can select via the *DivIDE Firmware* box. I use *FATware-0-12.bin*.

7. With the *SpecEmu* Options panel still open, click on the *Hard Disk Options* tab, click on the little '...' button at the end of the 'Unit 0' box and locate the .HDF file you made in step (5).

8. Exit *Options*. Your emulated Spectrum should reset and display the *DivIDE* screen shown in figure 8.1 below. Press any key.

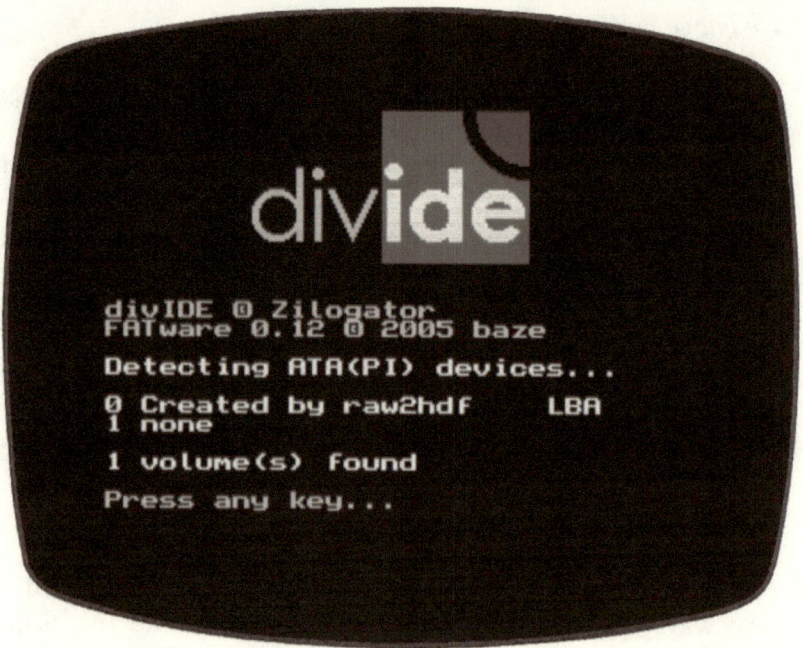

Fig 8.1 DivIDE boots, recognising a hard disk connected.

9. Your Spectrum should now go to BASIC. To see the contents

of your virtual hard disk, you need to generate an NMI (non-maskable interrupt). You can do so from the *Z80* menu.

10. You'll now be presented with a menu of your hard disk's contents. Select the file you'd like to use with your arrow keys and hit return. You are taken back to BASIC.

11. .TAP files selected will now load with the usual LOAD "" command. Saving isn't yet implemented in the FATware firmware, but – I gather – planned for a future update.

You can find out more about the *DivIDE* interface at *http://baze.au.com/divide*. Other mass storage devices you might like to explore are Gary Lancaster's *Spectrum +3e* and Sami Vehmaa's *ZXCF* interfaces.

Display

The Uncommitted Logic Array (ULA) chip used in the Spectrum did the job of handling input and output: scanning the keyboard, translating data from and into beeps and loading tones, and – crucially – converting the contents of the Spectrum's screen memory (the first 6912 bytes in the lower 16K of RAM, which – obviously – you knew already) into something that would display on a television. In layperson's terms a ULA chip is a 'semi-custom' device – a chip (in this case, manufactured by UK firm Ferranti) that can be set-up by the purchasing manufacturer (in this case, Sinclair) to perform a customised function. Using a ULA was essentially cheaper and faster than designing and creating your own chip from scratch, albeit the final product was less efficient than a bespoke manufactured device would have been. In Sinclair's first ZX computer – the ZX80 – 17 discrete logic chips were used; by adopting a ULA for its successor – the ZX81 – the overall chip count was reduced to just four chips, bringing both cost and power consumption (and, therefore, heat production) significantly down.

You can read more about the history and use of the ULA in Sinclair computers in Chris Smith's recent book, *The ZX Spectrum ULA: How to design a microcomputer*. Chris' work in reverse-engineering the Spectrum ULA was the key to being able to design an improved version of the chip – an idea first suggested by Andrew Owen in 2000 whilst working on his own Spectrum clone, *The ZX Spectrum SE* – which could effectively be dropped into an existing Spectrum in place of the old ULA and give it better graphics. The new ULA – 'ULAplus' – was designed by *Cheveron, Nikki, CSmith* and *KLP2*, and, in February 2011, completed as a Field-Programmable Gate Array (FPGA) core (the FPGA is a modern equivalent of the ULA, a chip designed to be configured by the customer once they've bought it) by Alessandro Dorigatti.

ULAplus (information about which can be found at *http://sites.google.com/site/ulaplus/*) expands the Spectrum's colour range from 16 to 256 colours. These are loaded in 'palettes' of 64 colours at a time. As with a normal Spectrum, you can still only have two colours per 8x8 pixel character (ie, colour clash is not eradicated by the new ULA) and the Spectrum's 256 x 192 resolution display is unchanged. The expanded colour range, therefore, improves rather than destroys the 'Spectrum look' on software designed to make use of its potential.

ULAplus is now supported by a number of emulators, including *SpecEmu, Spud* and *ZX SPIN*. To experience ULAplus in *SPIN*, you'll need a special beta version (0.7) not currently available from WoS. To download this, visit the ULAplus website mentioned earlier and follow the link on the left.

Enable ULAplus in *SPIN* by selecting the following: *Tools > Options > Display > Emulation*, then ticking the '64 Colour enhanced ULA' box. There are several games already available from the ULAplus website that take advantage of the chip's extra colours (there is also a list of enhanced games on WoS at *www.worldofspectrum.org/infoseek.cgi?regexp=^ULAplus+Support $&phrase*). My personal favourite is Jonathan Cauldwell's 2009 Christmas release *Batteries not precluded*, which is ridiculously addictive in its own right, but in the ULAplus version includes actually orange marmalade. Yes.

Modifying existing games is a simple matter of changing the palette before loading the game. You can do this for yourself using Andrew Owen's *Palette Editor* (the new version of Andrew's OpenSE BASIC features native support for the ULAplus, making palette creation even easier still) or the editors included in some emulators (*Tools > Palette Editor* in *SPIN*); there are also a number of palettes pre-prepared for specific titles (eg, *Dan Dare, Exolon* and

Commando) at the ULAplus website. Load these tape files into your Spectrum and then load in the game they were designed for.

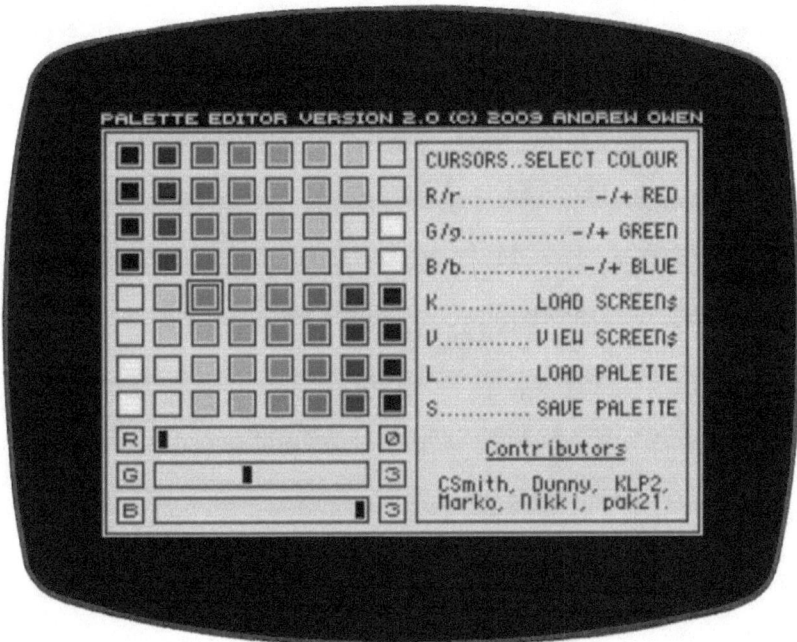

Fig 8.2 Palette Editor enables you to create your own colour palettes.

ULAplus also enables a 'HAM256' mode capable of displaying all 256 colours in a single screen. To do this, the palette has to be switched very rapidly. This technique is very dependent on the Spectrum's timings (just using one 64 colour palette for a screen is not), which is an area where emulators often vary. Support for this mode, therefore, is not currently consistent across the ULAplus emulators and – at the time of writing – *SpecEmu* is the best for displaying HAM images. Compare the *SpecEmu* screen in Figure 8.3 to the *ZX SPIN* screen in Figure 8.4.

ULAplus is not to be confused with the *Spec256* project mentioned in Chapter Seven (see the entry for *EmuZWin*). The hardware modifications required of that hypothetical upgrade would be essentially impossible. ULAplus is defined by its simplicity: a single chip to replace an existing one. In fact, the ULAplus design could actually have been implemented by Sinclair in 1982, albeit at considerable extra expense.

Fig 8.3 ULAplus HAM image displaying in SpecEmu.

Fig 8.4 ULAplus HAM image displaying in ZX SPIN.

Online connectivity

Until quite recently, all these attempts to 'update' the Spectrum with some of the advantages that modern hardware offers were missing a vital 21st century element: the Internet. Back in its day, the Spectrum did make its way onto the online world via the Prism VTX5000 Modem, however this device was for connecting to the Prestel Micronet – which no longer exists – and cannot be used as a way onto the modern Internet.

Putting the Spectrum online is more than about just forming a working connection between it and the net. Consider a modern web page: the graphics on it alone would exceed the Spectrum's normal memory, let alone the programming to translate HTML code into something that can be displayed on the Spectrum's screen. And, taking the Speccy's graphics resolution and colour limitations into account, the resulting ZX renditions of web pages might not be particularly pleasant to look at, even if the memory issues were dealt with (by including additional memory as part of a modem interface). An online Spectrum, therefore, is always going to be limited in the degree to which it can access the web without major other hardware modifications (which would, arguably, make it no longer a Spectrum).

That said, there *are* internet applications about today which *could* display perfectly well on a Spectrum. The modern internet relies very heavily on the syndication of text as content, which could be extracted by precise enough Spectrum software. The text of emails could be displayed, for example. Twitter users could read and send tweets. And the text content of many websites these days is available as RSS (Really Simple Syndication) feeds that could be used to recreate Spectrum-friendly pages (see, for example, *http://feeds.bbci.co.uk/news/rss.xml*). Potentially, even Facebook is doable if the software is clever enough to extract just the text updates (in a manner presumably not all that different from Facebook's own 'Facebook for every phone' application designed by the old *Snaptu* team). It's something of an irony, in fact, that the modern, better organised web of today is probably more compatible with the Spectrum than the rather messy web of ten years ago.

For Spectrum users, of course, there would be another big benefit to connecting up your Spectrum to the internet: access to the World of Spectrum archive. Locating and downloading (in an instant)

Spectrum software on WoS would be a very convenient way of putting Spectrum software back onto the real hardware.

Spectranet – a creation of *Winston* and very much a project under current development at the time of writing – is a serious attempt to get the Spectrum online. Details of this, a Spectrum ethernet interface, are available at *http://spectrum.alioth.net/doc/index.php* and you need to poke around in this site because it's not immediately obvious just how much information is available from it: not just the schematics and news of the production of pre-assembled boards to buy, but also a very comprehensive tutorial (*http://spectrum.alioth.net/doc/index.php/Spectranet:_Tutorial_1*).
In terms of software support, the project is still in its early stages, but I understand there is already a working Twitter client (a video of which is here: *www.youtube.com/watch?gl=GB&v=-ECnN7jdgA4*).

So far as emulation is concerned, *Spectranet* is the least emulated of the homebrew devices we've covered in this chapter. Currently, the device is only emulated by *Fuse* and then only in an uncompiled source release, the details of which can be obtained in this entry: *http://spectrum.alioth.net/doc/index.php/Current_events#Emulating_the_Spectranet*. Compiling an emulator from scratch is, I'm afraid, way too complicated for me. But Spectranet might well have made it into release version emulators by the time you read this, so check out the emulators page at WoS.

Chapter Nine
The ZX Spectrum on your portable device

One of the reasons why there's so much nostalgia and affection for the Spectrum is that those of us who grew up with it weren't just experiencing a first computer. Our kids today have experienced that without so much as batting an eyelid, for computers and the Internet to them are just part of the everyday background, like cars and television were for us. The Spectrum is special to us because it was our very own gateway into something new. Having a home computer back in the eighties – any home computer – was a bit like passing a personal point of no return. Things were never the same again. We were part of a revolution.

IT revolutions are somewhat taken for granted these days. In fact, they're pretty much expected. Windows – in particular, Windows 95 – could be touted as one. The Internet is undoubtedly another. Web 2.0 was a revolution that most people probably didn't realise was going on, except ask them how the internet was different when they first started using it and they'll realise it was a very different beast back in the days of Freeserve and AOL. USB didn't feel at all like a revolution when those little rectangular sockets first started appearing on our machines, but look at how data has become monetised since we started moving it around. Cloud computing is a revolution that's also very quietly underway, except infrastructure isn't quite up to fulfilling its promises yet. And then there's portable devices.

Portable devices such as the smartphone and tablet computer are probably the beginning of the end for the home PC as the mainstream access point to IT, and the start of computing invisibility. It isn't quite the computer-in-a-toaster sort of embeddedness that the futurologists used to talk about, but it's the first step. Ironically, it's not so much their actual portability as it is the way these devices facilitate some of those other revolutions – how we move our data about; how we access it; how we expect information to be delivered – that is their key significance. Portable devices are changing the way we think about computing and connectivity. By the time of the Spectrum's 50th anniversary, in fact, the term 'computer' will probably be out of circulation in everyday vocabulary. It will be everywhere and nowhere at the same time, our physical world pervaded by invisible layers of information we cannot imagine life without.

Always assuming, of course, a gigantic solar flare doesn't come along and muck everything up. Incidentally, I read once that a whole batch of Spectrum +2s got made up accidentally with electromagnetically shielded Z80 CPUs intended for military use (to protect their computers from the electromagnetic energy released in nuclear explosions), so – you never know – the Spectrum's usefulness might not be quite over yet if the sun does decide to throw something our way.

The PC's day isn't over yet by a long stretch – the council I work for has still to discover life after Windows XP and Internet Explorer 7; I think it's safe to say there's plenty of time before tablet computing arrives – but portable computing is a major game changer. I'm permitting myself the indulgence of this somewhat philosophical monologue on the topic because that's exactly what the home computer revolution of the eighties was. Just as our Spectrums were for us that little hint, that tiny insight of what was to come, so too are the portable devices of today. Things will never be quite the same again.

What, then, of Spectrum emulation? Already, there are several very well-developed emulators for portable devices. In fact, PC emulator development in recent years has largely slowed down, whilst portable emulator development has taken off in a big way. I will cover a few of these applications in brief detail here. At my disposal, I currently have a Nintendo DS, an iPod Touch and a Samsung Galaxy S mobile phone running Android 2.4. All of these are such small devices that the access they give to the Spectrum keyboard/joystick is very fiddly and I spend very little time using them for emulation. But I'm not going to highlight this as an insurmountable limitation because there are also, of course, tablets and their much bigger screens. I would imagine, in fact, that a rubber keys Spectrum keyboard displaying in the lower half of an iPad screen would be pretty close to life size. The high resolution of the iPad 3, in fact, offers the – I can't deny it – tempting prospect of a keyboard so photorealistic it almost looks like the real thing (bits of dust and all). I wonder how long it will be before 3D tablets come to pass...

Spectaculator by Jonathan Needle (iOS)

A good place to start is one of the emulators we've followed throughout the book. Available from the App Store, *Spectaculator* comes in a free and a paid for version, the paid for version currently costing £1.99.

Fig 9.1 Spectaculator on an iPhone.

Apple is well-known for the tight ship it runs in terms of what is and what isn't permissible in its App Store. This 'walled garden' approach has won it a good many critics; the PC equivalent would be only being able to download PC software from one online shop and one company therefore having the ultimate say in what you're allowed to run on your device. On the other hand, this also means Apple keeps a very close eye on quality. So far as Spectrum emulation is concerned, the key problem for App Store distribution is the intellectual ownership of Spectrum software. These old games might be ancient compared to modern software, but someone somewhere legally owns each and every one of them and making software available via the App Store that could access copies of them is, so far as Apple are concerned, an unacceptable legal risk. So you can't with *Spectaculator* download games from WoS. Instead, games are available to purchase via *Spectaculator* as properly licensed packs, and these are at the moment pretty limited.

The free version comes with eight games, all recently written titles with copyright 2010 or 2011. *Alter Ego* by Denis Grachev is a cheerful little collect-em-up. *Catch the Cash* by Tom Dalby – originally a 2011 Minigame competition entry – is a simple left/right-catch-falling-money-but-avoid-falling-bombs affair. *Crimbo* by Little Shop of Pixels involves Santa finding presents hidden by elves taking industrial action. And so on. They're all quite nice little games that manage to evoke that Spectrumy feeling sufficiently well that those with just a mild sense of nostalgia will probably be satisfied. You cannot enter Spectrum BASIC in the free version.

The paid for version features a few better-known titles, such as 3D Starstrike, Tau Ceti and a number of Jonathan Cauldwell games (see the Appendix B for details on a number of his creations). You can also enter 48K or 128K BASIC. The paid for version also features an in-app shop where you can download the aforementioned game packs. These are currently Zenobi Adventure Packs Vol. 1 and 2 (six games per pack at £1.49 each), a Realtime Games Pack containing StarStrike II and 3D Tank Duel (£0.69) and two free 'Modern Gems' packs – six/seven games per pack, the first of which comprises the games that come with the free version of *Spectaculator*. You can also buy a couple of individual games from the in-app store: Dynamite Dan II and Frank N. Stein, both at £0.69 each. And that's it. If you were hoping to play specific titles on this app, then, you're likely to be sorely disappointed.

But hey. This is only £2 we're talking about for the basic emulator. And it does present a legitimate way round the Apple restrictions if you want to experience Spectrum emulation on your iDevice (without jailbreaking it). And it does also raise the profile of modern Spectrum games. And – as an author of a couple of Spectrum text adventures myself – I can't say I disapprove of Zenobi making a little money on their back catalogue either. And the range could, of course, grow. So far as emulation is concerned, the implementation of the Spectrum appears flawless and the onscreen joystick is not too bad at all (I generally find non-tactile controllers a little difficult to get on with, but this one was fairly easy to pick up and the way it's presented in landscape mode is very unobtrusive). The app is very well organised, with games organised alphabetically; each has its own instructions screen plus there's a link for each title to its page at The Tipshop website.

ZX Spectrum: Elite Collection by Elite Systems (iOS)

Elite Systems were a very big name in Spectrum computing back in the eighties, particularly famous for arcade conversions such as Commando and Ghosts 'n' Goblins. Elite's implementation of iPod/Phone/Pad Spectrum emulation is not a great deal different from *Spectaculator's* except their marketing is focused more on selling the games than on selling the emulator. The Elite Collection is, in fact, one of quite a number of Elite releases in the App Store, the vast majority of these being individual Spectrum games (Manic Miner, Barbarian, Skool Daze, to name but a few) selling at £1.49 each. Given that The Elite Collection comes complete with thirteen games for £1.99, it's therefore quite good value for money by comparison. These aren't unknown games either: Elite's own Grand National, Buggy Boy, Frank Bruno's Boxing, Roller Coaster, Beyond the Ice Palace, Batty, Kokotoni Wilf and Battleships, plus Durell's Saboteur, Saboteur II, Turbo Esprit and Harrier Attack. You also get Chuckie Egg.

Having purchased the app, you can then buy further individual titles at £0.69 each (many of them the £1.49 titles if bought outside of the app) or collections or games (six per pack) at £1.49 per collection. There's quite a range of in-app games to download, with Gremlin Graphics, Hewson and Palace prominent as featured publishers. A far greater range than *Spectaculator,* then, and very slickly presented too. There's also an in-game plea for the owners of Spectrum games to approach Elite if they would like their game(s) included in a future collection, so every indication that the range will continue to grow.

Emulation seems very good and the controls are customisable so you can find the system that works best for you. But, so far as I can tell, there's neither access to Sinclair BASIC nor keyboard support in the Elite emulator. No adventure games likely to be included in future collections, then, unless that changes.

Marvin by Richard (Android)

Of course, the Android market takes a rather different, hands-off approach to the legal issues discussed earlier than Apple does. Android apps are as free to download from WoS as PCs are, so the issue of paying for games or game packs doesn't arise – at least, not so far (it's always possible that the game owners currently in agreement with Elite could ask Martijn to remove their titles from distribution if a similar attempt were made to sell on the Android market as has been made on the Apple market). Marvin, therefore, is a different sort of emulator, much more focused on the machine. It offers access to BASIC in both 48K and 128K mode and you can save things done there (or in a game) as a snapshot file (there's no facility to save as a tape file, but you could always transfer the snapshot to a PC emulator and sort that out from there).

In addition to loading games you've transferred to the phone yourself, there's also an option to connect direct to WoS and search the database in-app, then download your selected title straight to your device. This works flawlessly.

What doesn't work flawlessly, unfortunately, are the controls. Whilst the in-game joystick works as well as can be expected for a non-tactile device, the fire button – placed in the top-right corner of the screen in landscape mode – is perilously close to the Android back button; an assertive return of fire can end up exiting the emulator to the Android home screen.

I also had issues with the keyboard. Whilst letters and numbers seemed to work well, anything involving the CAPS SHIFT key appeared to be a matter of pure luck. This is problematic if you ever need to delete anything. Of course, one of the problems with writing an Android app is all the variations between the different Android devices. There's no such thing as a standard Android screen size, so it might be that Marvin's keyboard works perfectly on – say – an HTC device. On my Samsung Galaxy S, however, it more or less refused to work.

But *Marvin* is free and the games are free, and so long as you remember to rotate your screen clockwise instead of anti-clockwise then your arcade gaming experiences should be as good as any of the Apple offerings, albeit at considerably less money.

Speccy by Marat Fayzullin (Android)

Speccy, like *Spectaculator*, began life as a PC emulator. You'll see from Chapter Seven that it gave me a few problems. What, then, of the Android version?

In fact, this is the one of the most comprehensive smartphone Spectrum emulators available. The various menus are a little on the complicated side and the frequent requests in the free version to click on one of the ads or purchase the paid for version (which will cost you £3.99) can become a little distracting; once you've got your head around the various options, however, you'll be pleasantly surprised at just how much you can do with this app. Supported models include all UK Spectrums, the Timex-Sinclair TS2068 and Timex Portugal TC2048, the Pentagon and the Scorpion. Plug-in hardware supported includes the Kempston and AMX mouse, Fuller sound, the ZX Printer, the Sinclair IF 1, the MGT Disciple/+D and all three Multifaces. Pretty impressive. The emulator has support for .TZX files and it even sports a built-in debugger.

Loading games is a little more complicated on *Speccy* than on *Marvin*. There's no connection to WoS, so you have to move games across from your PC to your phone storage (you could always, of course, get them onto your phone via *Marvin*). Joystick control is okay, and in landscape mode you get a nice overlay showing controls just prominent enough to see them without obscuring the enlarged screen. A little keyboard overlay works in much the same way – it's a tad on the hard side to make out the keys, but they seem to work very smoothly – none of the key press problems that I encountered in *Marvin*.

An extra curiosity in *Speccy* is its tilt joystick, allowing you to control movement within a game by tilting your device. This actually works surprisingly well, technically; the problem is it's terrible as a control device for most Spectrum games. Also, a bug I seemed to encounter when using the tilt joystick was that the keyboard appeared to stop registering key presses (although I didn't stay in tilt joystick mode long enough for that actually to become a problem). It's a novelty that doesn't really work, but kudos to Marat for giving it a go (and just because it doesn't work for *existing* Spectrum games, doesn't mean to say that new titles couldn't be written with this in mind).

ZXdroid by Dmitry Rodin (Android)

ZXdroid is a port of Philip Kendal's *Fuse* (see Chapter Seven). As you'd expect from an emulator as well developed as *Fuse* is, there's a very wide range of computers covered: all the UK Spectrums; all the Timex Spectrum clones; all the Pentagon and Scorpion variants. It also emulates the Spectrum SE and the Spectrum +3e.

As with *Speccy,* games are loaded from your phone rather than direct from WoS. Control is via either a directional arrows pad or keyboard and I missed *Speccy's* always onscreen button to activate the keyboard; in *ZXdroid,* you have to change the input method via the main menu, which can result in a lot of too-ing and fro-ing when starting the game requires a keyboard press. I also found the arrows pad extremely hard to manipulate: both the directional controls and the fire button are located on the left-hand side, so that your right hand has to cross the screen to use fire. Also, it appears to be impossible to fire whilst pressing a directional control, which is a major drawback.

ZXdroid is free and ad-supported. In portrait mode, the ad sits nicely at the bottom of the screen, however in landscape mode it takes up room below the main display at the right of the screen. This, plus the fact that the controls do not overlay the display as they tend to in other emulators, make the screen display in landscape only very slightly bigger than it is in portrait, effectively wiping out one of the key advantages to implementing a Spectrum emulator on a smartphone device.

ZXDS by Patrik Rak (Nintendo DS)

The pixel resolution of the Nintendo DS is 256 by 192 – exactly the resolution of the Spectrum's display area (ie, minus the border). Which makes this portable console a perfect fit for Spectrum emulation.

Like the DS itself, *ZXDS* has been around for a few years now, but is still being updated. Unlike installing an app on a smartphone, getting *ZXDS* will require a bit of work (and expense, if you've never installed homebrew software on your DS before). But it's worth it. The physical controller of the DS coupled with the emulator's ease of use make this – in my opinion – the best overall portable Spectrum experience to be had.

First of all, you're going to need a homebrew card for your DS. I'm not going to go into the details of this here because cards and their operating systems change; also, there are different rules and products according to which version of the DS you have. I run my version of *ZXDS* on a DS Lite, which you can typically pick up on Ebay now for under £40; although this version of the DS has a smaller screen than later versions, there are fewer firmware issues with this model (Nintendo started pushing firmware updates over the internet from the DSi onwards) plus I like its compatibility with GBA games. I run *ZXDS* on an *Acekard 2*, a 'SLOT 1' card (SLOT 1 being the place where you insert normal DS cards) with its own Micro SD slot. I have a 2GB Micro SD card inserted in that, which is more than enough for my Spectrum emulation needs. I transfer Spectrum software from my PC onto the SD card using one of those little USB card readers that you can sometimes pick up at the pound shop.

For information about DS cards, a good starting place is *http://en.wikipedia.org/wiki/Nintendo_DS_storage_devices*.

ZXDS is free and available from *http://zxds.raxoft.cz*. What you get when you load it up is the Spectrum display on the upper of the DS's two screens and the keyboard on the lower. On the issue of the keyboard, the nature of the DS's lower touch screen is such that it works best when you use a stylus on it (as opposed to modern smartphone touch screens, which require a finger touch – great for most smartphone uses, but lousy when it comes to precision); although the Spectrum keyboard on *ZXDS* is very small, therefore, being able to access it using the stylus makes it by far the easiest of the keyboards discussed so far and therefore the best for playing adventure games (or programming, if ever the desire should take you whilst you're out and about).

Across the top of the lower screen are *ZXDS*'s control panel icons. To load a game, select *IO* and then *LOAD FILE*. *ZXDS* comes with its own *GAMES* and *DEMOS* folders for you to drop your Spectrum files into from your PC, but there's also an *ONLINE* option for you to select if your DS is wireless enabled. Choose this, and you get presented with five online destinations. The last of these is WoS, where you can browse and download from the entire WoS database: find the game you're after, select it and play; it's that simple.

But that's not all. The other online destinations include The Tipshop and The RZX Archive: you can download both POKEs and RZX demonstrations using *ZXDS*. As I write this, in fact, Daley Thompson is getting cheered on by the crowd through each of the first five of his ten Decathlon events. Happy memories.

Fig 9.2 ZXDS, shown here playing an RZX recording of Jonathan Cauldwell's 'Battery's not precluded'.

ZXDS supports 48K and 128K games plus Pentagon software. It will load all formats of snapshot file and supports both .TAP and .TZX files (and the emulator's own .PZX tape format). You can save out as a .SZX snapshot file (which you could convert to a .TZX file later on your PC if you wanted to). There's also a very comprehensive help system: tap the *HELP* icon and everything you tap after that is explained in the upper screen. Tap *HELP* again to turn this off.

What really makes *ZXDS* for me, though, is the ease with which you can use it for gaming. The physical controller (which you can map onto any of the Spectrum joystick standards) makes game control the best that I've ever experienced for Spectrum games – better than keyboard control on the Spectrum itself and (by a very considerable margin) better than anything so far available on smartphone devices. *ZXDS* is a gamer's emulator, and it's perfect. The only improvement suggestion I would make is support for ULAplus (see Chapter Eight); somehow, it feels like this would work here extremely well.

The Art of Spectrum

www.flickr.com/photos/79238217@N06/

Appendix A
About the ZX Spectrum

This rather lengthy appendix combines a number of different articles I wrote for ZXF and Micro Mart with a few revisions and additional text here and there. An overview of the Spectrum and its significance, it's included more for leisure reading than any attempt to be a complete Spectrum reference (which would require a whole book in its own right – and a lengthy one, at that); nonetheless, I hope it has some use as a reference source for the mildly curious. It begins by looking at some of the main features of the Spectrum as a cultural phenomenon and then presents an overview of the key dates in the Spectrum's evolution. A list of further reading and web links is presented at the end for those who would like to delve further into the detail.

What made the Spectrum Britain's best-selling and most influential home computer?

Price

Of all factors, cost was probably the most important in the Spectrum's success. At under £200, the Spectrum was a genuine price breakthrough for a computer of its power, and later the cost of a 48K model would drop still further, from £179 to £125. Of course its predecessor, the ZX81, had also been a cheap computer and had sold well (without the success of the ZX81, there might never have been a Spectrum) but over the ZX81 the Spectrum had more memory, better graphics, *colour* graphics, sound and looked and felt better. The rubber keyboard might well have attracted criticism at the time, but it brought the price down, was a definite improvement over the ZX81's flat membrane overlay and – incidentally –

introduced new technology which would be used in many future devices. The Spectrum was not just a cheap computer, therefore, it was a cheap *and desirable* computer.

'Educational'

Sinclair was keen to promote the Spectrum as a powerful educational tool. The message was heard by parents up and down the land. For those that didn't hear it direct from Sinclair, their teenagers would be only too happy to repeat it for their benefit. Of course gaming was the real reason why most of those kids wanted Spectrums; would the machine have sold so well so quickly if it had been marketed as such, however?

Specifications

It would, of course, be a mistake to claim the Spectrum represented the state of the art in computer technology for the time. Its colour clash, for example, would become derided by the users of other machines in competitive playground banter. But how many of us Spectrum wannabes even noticed colour clash before we got to know our machines? When your mate showed you Sabre Wulf on his new computer he'd just been bought for his birthday (because it was 'educational') were you thinking to yourself what a turn off the occasional spots of colour clash were? Well, I know I wasn't. Hi-res graphics, colour, sound and that enormous 48K memory were all you needed to know.

Aesthetics

The design of the Spectrum - by Rick Dickinson, who won a Design Council award for his design for the ZX81 – was quite unique. It looked good then and it looks good now. Can you honestly say the same of other computers of the era? At the time they might have looked more like how we felt computers should look, but now they look just dated and, well, yellow. Legend has it that Alan Sugar wanted his rival product, the Amstrad CPC64 to resemble a "real computer, similar to what someone would see being used to check them in at the airport for their holidays", and for the machine to not look like "a pregnant calculator" – clearly a reference to the

Spectrum's design. As a design strategy, Lord Sugar's approach probably wasn't far off the mark in terms of what people wanted at the time. He applied it to the Spectrum +2 very successfully; the machine sold well and arguably sustained the Spectrum software market well beyond its natural shelf life. But now – thirty years later – the original Spectrum design looks bold, compact and stylish where the later Amstrad models look somehow clunky and dated. It would be many years before Apple 'revolutionised' the IT world in its iMac with the novel idea that what a computer looked like was important. Sinclair was there first.

The ZXF stand at the Micro Mart Computer Fair, 2003. Could have done better.

During my time editing ZXF and writing articles for Micro Mart, I was invited by the Retro Mart columnist Shaun Bebbington to display at the Retro stand at the Micro Mart Computer Fair at Birmingham NEC. If I'm to be completely honest, my representation of the Spectrum that day was a little bit pitiful: I had one spare TV to hand – which I connected up to one of my

Spectrum pluses (not even a rubber-keyed Spectrum) – and a laptop running an old DOS Spectrum emulator (because it was too slow to run a Windows emulator). Sandwiched between the QL User Group's frankly overwhelming army of computers (none of which, incidentally looked like a QL) and Colin Piggot's mightily impressive Sam Coupé demonstrations (the output of his SAM soundcard was probably audible at Birmingham New Street) the UK's most popular home computer of the 1980s deserved a much better presence in that hall than I was resourced to give it. The enduring memory of the event for me, however, was the number of people of my age who, on walking past the display, reached out to brush their fingers across the Spectrum's keyboard. This display of fondness for the tactile memory of the Spectrum's design – a dimension of our sensory experience of interface often overlooked – lives with me as evidence that the Spectrum was way more than just its specifications or price or software catalogue.

Games

Ten thousand of them. Amongst them titles you just *had* to have. Amongst them classics considered now to have created design principles coders continue to follow to this day. Manic Miner, Sabrewulf, The Hobbit, Daley Thompson's Decathalon, Knight Lore, Skool Daze, 3D Starstrike, Trashman, Elie, Fairlight, Match Day, Tau Ceti, Way of the Exploding Fist, The Great Escape, MOVIE, Exolon, Head Over Heels, Cybernoid... the list is endless (and we haven't even touched on the coin-op conversions). And they're still being made today: check out Appendix B for reviews of a selection of modern Spectrum titles.

Perhaps most important of all was that Spectrum games could be copied - all it took was a tape-to-tape stereo, and most of us had access to one of those. Sure, it was illegal - and we all occasionally spent time fretting over those stories about the police raiding some-teenager-somewhere's collection of C90s - but the casette of copied games represented two important things: free software for your Speccy in the receiving and mates in the giving. At the time, these were pretty much the only boxes in a teenage boy's life that needed ticking. Apart from girls. But two out of three wasn't bad.

Magazines

Whichever your personal favourite was, once the Spectrum magazines transformed themselves from boring type-in anthologies to funky social commentators, a new cultural dimension was added to the whole computer ownership thing. You couldn't take your Spectrum to school, but a copy of CRASH slipped into the bag easily. On the issue of making friends, the magazines provided important information on *which* games were the most popular. Well-chosen titles and a tape-to-tape recorder didn't just equal friends, you see; it equalled *status*.

BASIC

With its built-in BASIC, the ease with which the Spectrum could be programmed created something of a revolution in 'bedroom programming' - not just the oft-noted phenomena of a few youngsters creating games to sell to Ocean for the price of a sports car and a Sonny Crockett jacket (if you believe the advert...), but a much wider number of users who, every now and again, just liked to dip their toe in and dabble. Instantly on power-up, the BASIC language was there waiting for you. It took just two lines of code to demonstrate to the average schoolboy what that meant and to hint at what was achievable:

```
10 PRINT "hello"
20 GOTO 10
```

Talking about the Spectrum on a BBC documentary, Clive Sinclair - who, legend has it, was inspired to create the ZX80 after seeing the enjoyment his son got from programming a TRS-80 - remarked, "we realised obviously there would be a games aspect, but the first appeal was to people who wanted to get their hands on one and do some programming themselves. Which they loved doing. I mean, children took to that dramatically. And it's a bit sad today that that really isn't available to them."

It was really the first two years or so of the Spectrum's life that can perhaps most accurately be referred to as the 'BASIC era'. Many of Sinclair's early own-brand software titles were written in BASIC; magazines of the period leaned heavily on type-ins; and an endless array of BASIC teachyourselfs jostled for your attention at the book shop. Although the main focus of Spectrum usage did shift rapidly to games, programming as an essential part of the Spectrum Experience was never entirely lost - *Your Sinclair*, for example, continued to include its regular 'Program Pitstop' collection of novelty type-ins right up to its 'Big Final Issue' in 1993.

Spectrum BASIC was in fact the third incarnation of Sinclair BASIC, following versions created for the Sinclair ZX80 and ZX81 computers. All three were developed by a company called *Nine Tiles Software* - not actually Sinclair at all; John Grant wrote the ZX80's *Integer BASIC* in a meagre 4K of memory, and Cambridge mathematician Steven Vickers wrote the BASICs for the ZX81 and then the Spectrum (in 8K and 16K respectively). What made Sinclair BASIC special? Technically speaking, it wasn't the best on offer - its ability to loop was restricted to FOR...NEXT and GOTO, and its handling of sub-routines was even more, well, basic. Where it shone, however, was in its handling of user errors: immediate feedback via in-built syntax routines - which not only rejected incorrectly formatted statements, but also highlighted where the errors were in your code - made Spectrum BASIC very easy to learn through trial and error. And colour and sound were accessed through a small number of conceptually very straightforward commands - INK, PAPER, BRIGHT, etc (compare this, for example, to the complicated system of PEEKs POKEs and CHR$ stuff on the C64) - making graphics and music extremely accessible. Throw in a very readable BASIC programming manual by Vickers and Robin Bradbeer (the typically well-thumbed condition of copies on ebay is testament to the use that this book got put to) and the end result was a system very much orientated towards persuading the beginner there was a great that deal they - *they* - were able to achieve with it. The bedroom programmer was born. Once you'd mastered BASIC, the next logical step was to assembly language and the speed and power of machine code. The strength of the British game producing industry today is often attributed to the easy route into programming offered by the Spectrum.

In BASIC lies the Spectrum's legacy, and also its irony: we told our parents that a Spectrum would be good for our education, when really we wanted it for the games, but even the most die-hard gamer couldn't avoid learning just a little about BASIC; it turns out, you see, that all ended up getting educated after all.

Key Sinclair/Spectrum dates from the last 30 years.

1982

- *23 April.* Clive Sinclair announces the launch of the ZX Spectrum at the Earls Court Computer Show. The new machine will sell at £125 for 16K RAM and £175 for 48K; orders will be delivered in 'two weeks'.
- *April.* First issue of *Sinclair User* (ECC Publications Ltd.).
- *May.* First issue *Sinclair Programs* (ECC Publications Ltd.).
- *July.* Spectrums start in production after a problem with the ULA chip is resolved.
- *October.* Advertising Standards Authority upholds complaints against Spectrum ads due to "appalling delays" in delivery.
- *Month unknown.* Rick Dickinson, designer of the Spectrum, wins a British Design Council award for his ZX81 design.

1983

- *January.* Sinclair Research valued at £136m; N M Rothschild & Son purchase 10% of the company, making Clive £13.6m.
- *February.* Computer division of Sinclair Research moves into specially converted premises at 25 Willis Road, Cambridge (previously Barker & Wadsworth mineral water bottling factory).
- *March.* Clive Sinclair wins *Young Businessman of the Year* award.
- *May.* The price of the Spectrum is dropped to £99.95 for the 16K model and £129.95 for the 48K model.
- *June.* Clive Sinclair is knighted.
- *July.* ZX Interface 1 and Microdrives launched (£49.95 each, but £79.95 when bought together).
- *September.* Interface 2 ROM cartridge/joystick interface launched (£19.95). Sinclair flat-screen pocket TV launched at £79.95.
- *Autumn.* Manic Miner, the "definitive Spectrum platform game" released by Bug-Byte Software for £5.95.

1984

- *Early 1984.* The software company *Imagine* goes bust, the whole

thing being captured (somewhat spectacularly) by a BBC documentary (*www.youtube.com/watch?v=Yt9BsZCifgU*)
- *January.* Sinclair QL launched at £399.
- *January.* First issue of *Your Spectrum* (Sportscene Specialist Press).
- *February.* First issue of *CRASH* (Newsfield Publications)
- *May.* First reported delivery of a QL to a customer - returned within a week. ASA upholds complaints on QL delivery claims.
- *October.* Spectrum+ launches at £179.95

1985

- *10 January.* C5 vehicle launched at £399.
- *20 January.* Spectrum+ price dropped to £129.95, 48K rubber keys Spectrum discontinued. Upgrade of Spectrum to Spectrum+ offered for £30 (and a DIY kit for £20).
- *February.* QL production suspended.
- *March.* Production faults on C5 halt production for three weeks. Unemployed teenagers hired to drive C5s around London, Manchester, Birmingham & Leeds.
- *14 April.* C5 banned in Holland.
- *25 April.* ASA upholds complaints on unsubstantiated claims in C5 adverts.
- *April.* Hoover cut C5 workforce to 12 from 100 & production from 1000/week to 100.
- *2 June.* Sinclair Vehicles confirms it is looking to sell company.
- *17 June.* Robert Maxwell announces rescue bid for Sinclair Research, which has £15m debts (but aborts in August).
- *13 August.* Hoover stops C5 production.
- *24 August.* QL price cut from to £199.95.
- *August.* Final issue of *Sinclair Prpgrams*.
- *23 September.* The Spectrum 128K is unveiled at Barcelona Computer Fair, a result of joint venture between Investronica and Sinclair. The machine would not launch in the UK until the new year, due to a large number of unsold Spectrum+ machines which Sinclair hoped would sell over the Christmas period.
- *6 November.* TPD Ltd (ex-Sinclair Vehicles) goes into voluntary liquidation with debts of £6.4m.

1986

- *January.* Your Spectrum relaunched as *Your Sinclair*.
- *13 February.* Spectrum 128K launched in UK for £179.95.
- *7 April.* Amstrad pays £5m for all rights to existing Sinclair computer products, and commits £11m for outstanding orders and work in progress.
- *3 September.* The first Amstrad Spectrum, the *Spectrum +2*, launches at the PCW show at Olympia. This will sell for £159.

1987

- *30 May.* The industry gets its first look at the *Spectrum +3*, the first Spectrum to feature a built-in (3") disk drive. The machine is launched in the summer for £250, but soon has its price cut to £199.
- *August.* Sir Clive Sinclair launches his new portable computer, the *Z88* at the PCW show (under the new company *Cambridge Computers Ltd*).
- *August.* Format magazine launches to support users of the MGT Disciple/Plus D disk interfaces (& later the SAM Coupé).

1988

- *Late Autumn.* The Spectrum +2A is introduced to replace Amstrad's original +2. The new machine – essentially a +3 but with a tape deck in place of the disk drive – is soon criticised for its poor compatibility with older Spectrum software.

1989

- *December.* Miles Gordon Technology (MGT) launch their 'spiritual successor' to the Spectrum, the SAM Coupé. The late launch means that it misses the Christmas market. A ROM problem also means replacement chips have to be sent out.
- *Month unknown.* The Pentagon (unofficial Spectrum clone) appears in the USSR.

1990

- *June.* MGT go into receivership.
- *August.* Alan Miles and Bruce Gordon purchase MGT's assets and form SAM Computers (SAMCo) Ltd to continue marketing the SAM Coupé.

1991

- *30 July.* Z80 (Shareware Spectrum emulator for the PC) released.
- *September.* Newsfield, publisher of *CRASH* magazine, goes into liquidation.
- *November.* Europress Publications buy Newsfield's assests; *CRASH* returns after a month's absence.

1992

- *April.* Final issue of *CRASH* as Europress sell it off to Emap. The title is incorporated into Sinclair User.
- *15 July.* SAMCo goes into liquidation.
- *November.* Stock from SAMCo bought by West Coast Computers; SAM Coupé re-released as SAM Élite.
- *Month unknown.* Scorpion (unofficial Spectrum clone) 'launched' in Russia.

1993

- *April.* Work starts on *Warajevo* (PC Spectrum emulator) in war-torn city of Sarajevo to distract the authors from the horrors of the Bosnian War.
- *May.* Final issue of Sinclair User.
- *July.* *Dalek Attack,* the final 'commercial release' for the Spectrum goes on sale.
- *September.* *Your Sinclair* finishes with 'The Big Final Issue' (issue 93).
- *December.* comp.sys.sinclair (CSS) news-group opens.

1995

- *30 November.* The *World of Spectrum* website (WoS) launches.

1997

- February. TZX ('virtual cassette') format for Spectrum emulators developed by Tomaz Kac. The name TZX was suggested by Radovan Garabik in a discussion on CSS.

1999

- *July.* First version of Fuse (Unix Spectrum emulator) released.

2000

- December. WoS Forums opens.

2001

- *December.* First version of *Spectaculator* (Windows Spectrum emulator) released.

2003

- *March. Cronosoft*, a new commercial label for 8-bit software launches with its first Spectrum release, *Egghead in Space*.

2004

- *January. Retro Gamer magazine* launches. Marking its hundredth issue in 2012 and currently edited by Darran Jones, the publication has dedicated many thousands of words to the Spectrum, including the cover-mounted *Your Sinclair Issue 94* special in November 2004.

2007

- *July.* BSkyB announce a takeover of *Amstrad* for £125m. Sinclair Computers intellectual property now belongs to them.

Further reading and weblinks

Books

www.worldofspectrum.org holds a number of key Spectrum books and manuals published during its commercial life. Unless otherwise indicated, all of these titles can be obtained in PDF format from the WoS books page: *ftp://ftp.worldofspectrum.org/pub/sinclair/books/* Downloadable titles of note include:

- *ZX Spectrum Introduction* (the original orange introductory booklet that came with rubber-keyed Spectrums).

- *Sinclair ZX Spectrum BASIC* Programming by Steven Vickers (edited by Robin Bradbeer). A web version of this important book is located at *www.worldofspectrum.org/ZXBasicManual/* The manual is also incorporated into *BASin's* help system.

- *ZX Spectrum+ User Guide* (The Dorling Kindersley guide that shipped with the Spectrum+ and Spectrum+ 128).

- *ZX Spectrum+ 128 Introduction* booklet.

- ZX Spectrum +2, +3 and +2A Manuals. The Amstrad manuals take a great deal of their material from the original BASIC programming manual and are regarded as technically very good guides.

- The Dorling Kindersley *Step-by-Step* books one to four.

- *The Spectrum Programmer* by S. M. Gee. One of the Granada series of books (my personal favourite).

- *An Expert Guide to the Spectrum* by Mike James. Another excellent Granada title.

- *Spectrum Machine Language for the Absolute Beginner.* The Melbourne House Spectrum machine code bible edited by William Tang.

- *The Complete Spectrum ROM Disassembly* by Dr Ian Logan and Dr Frank O'Hara. Another Melbourne House Spectrum bible for serious coders.

And many, many more.

Since the Spectrum's commercial life ended, there have been further publications about it worth reading. These include:

- *The ZX Spectrum Book 1982 – 199X* by Andrew Rollings, a celebration of over 200 games with a foreword by Clive Sinclair. A PDF scan of this title is also available from WoS.

- *The ZX Spectrum ULA: How to design a microcomputer* by Chris Smith, the culmination of his work on reverse enginerring the Spectrum's ULA and available to buy from *www.zxdesign.info/book*

- *The ZX Spectrum/Commodore 64 Book* by Imagine publishing. A collection of Retro Gamer articles on the two great eighties micros. And possibly some sort of attempt to broker peace... www.imagineshop.co.uk/index.php/catalog/product/view/id/1824/

Video

YouTube is full to bursting with 8-bit gaming videos. If you watch nothing else, make sure you check out the ten very enjoyable chapters of the *Your Sinclair Rock 'n' Roll Years* documentary by Nick Humphries, charting the major Spectrum events of the years 1982 to 1990. There's even a Christmas special (Nick rather likes Christmas). *www.ysrnry.co.uk/tvprog/downloads.htm*

Other videos of note include:

- *Commercial Breaks*. A fascinating BBC documentary following the crash of Imagine Software Ltd in 1984 and its subsequent purchase by Ocean; a real window into the Spectrum software world. *www.youtube.com/watch?v=Yt9BsZCifgU*

- *Making the most of the Micro*. Not Sinclair specific, but still wonderful to watch: the BBC's original series aimed at improving the nation's computer literacy. These have been uploaded in parts to *www.youtube.com/user/MicroManMachine*

- *Thumb Candy*. A Chanel 4 documentary from 2000 on the history of video games, now widely regarded as a classic in its own right. Presented by Ian Lee, the whole film is currently online at http://www.youtube.com/watch?v=UAo4CZTGFQQ

- *Micro Men*. This wonderful BBC4 dramatisation of the relationship between Sir Clive Sinclair and Chris Curry exceeded all my expectations when it was released in 2009. Currently online at *www.youtube.com/watch?v=sIcAyFVK0gE*

- *La Puerta de Sinclair (Sinclair's Gate)*. A fantasy short from Akton Films about a parallel dimension in which Spectrum monsters rule. Yes. I helped write the English subtitles for this. *www.youtube.com/watch?v=BUO5l2uJ4Xc*

Our heroes dive for cover behind the wall from Arkanoid, fleeing pursuing eight bit monsters in 'La Puerta de Sinclair'. Or is that the wall from Batty? Oh dear...

Weblinks

Apart from WoS, there are literally thousands of web pages about the ZX Spectrum. Here are a few to get you started on your web travels.

Planet Sinclair *www.nvg.ntnu.no/sinclair/*

Before WoS became the supremo web phenomena that it is, there was *Planet Sinclair*. A site packed full of all products Sinclair – including his previous computers and latter inventions, from the ill-fated C5 right up to the Wheelchair Drive Unit in 2002 – you can read here also a biography of the man himself and browse a very detailed year-by-year breakdown of events (a lot of the 80s information in my own timeline was informed by this resource). Maintained by Chris Owen.

CRASH Online *www.crashonline.org.uk*

A website set up to celebrate CRASH magazine (my own favourite of the Spectrum mags), *CRASH Online*, maintained by Matthew Wilson, contains loads of web-converted articles as well as other information on the early years of CRASH as a mail order catalogue. A number of editions of CRASH have also been converted to Kindle format for you to download.

Your Sinclair The Rock 'n' Roll Years *www.ysrnry.co.uk*

In a similar vein, *Your Sinclair The Rock 'n' Roll Years* is a tribute to Your Sinclair, the longest lasting of the Spectrum mags. Maintained by Nick Humphries, expect masses of web-converted articles as well loads of extra features, including his yearly advert calendar treat and his look at the Retro Gamer YS special in 2004. Nick is also responsible for the TV documentary mentioned earlier.

Your Spectrum *www.users.globalnet.co.uk/~jg27paw4/*

Of course, before Your Sinclair became Your Sinclair, it was Your Spectrum. The 21 issues of the YS predecessor can be found here. Maintained by Jim Grimwood.

Sinclair User Magazine Online *www.sincuser.f9.co.uk*

And that only leaves Sinclair User. Maintained by Dave Foreman, SUMO offers up the same serving of web-converted articles – organised on an issue by issue basis.

The Tipshop *www.the-tipshop.co.uk*

I've already mentioned Gerard Sweeney's *The Tipshop*, but it's worth mentioning again as an indispensable source of cheats and POKEs for a massive range of Spectrum games.

comp.sys.sinclair
http://groups.google.com/forum/?fromgroups#!forum/comp.sys.sinclair

The original Sinclair discussion group – which covers the other Sinclair computers as well as the Spectrum – is still alive and well, now hosted by Google Groups.

The TZX Vault *www.tzxvault.org*

Steve Brown's archive of Spectrum games in .TZX format is also noteworthy for its archive of +D and other disk format images.

WoS weblinks *www.worldofspectrum.org/links.html*

For yet more weblinks, WoS maintains a comprehensive list of Spectrum websites.

Appendix B
Some modern Spectrum games

This is a selection of my own software reviews for new Spectrum titles released during the period 2002 – 2007; they were published in *Micro Mart*, *Your Sinclair* issue 94 and *ZXF*. There continue to be lots of new Spectrum games being released every year by extremely talented programmers. To hunt them down, click on the 'What's new' link on the front page of www.worldofspectrum.org and scroll down the entries looking for items tagged 'Brand new software'.

Abe's Mission – Escape by TCG
(ZXF, Christmas 2003)

So how cool is this? A PlayStation game converted to run on a Spectrum. Yes. Well, sort of. 'Abe's Mission – Escape' is based on the Abe games (*Abe's Oddysee* and *Abe's Exoddus*) by G T Interactive for the PS One (as it's now called) and was originally an entry for the Russian 'Your Game' competition in ABZAC Magazine in 2002. Now it's been translated into Czech and English by Total Computer Gang (TCG) programmers Wixet and zOOm in collaboration with Sweet Factory of C15 and released in MB-02, D40/80 and good old .TAP formats. A fairly impressive piece of joint working, then.

To get Abe's Mission to work, you'll need to run your (128K) Spectrum - real or emulated, of course - in USR 0 mode, which is a simple matter of entering 128 BASIC and typing 'USR 0' (and ENTER, obviously): the Spectrum will appear to reset into 48K mode; just type LOAD "" and start your tape. Select English language from the intro page and you're away.

In Abe's Mission - Escape, our hero, floor-waxing employee of the year at the Oddworld RaptureFarms meat processing plant, overhears a conversation in which the true ingredients of *New'n'tasty* Scrab Cakes and Paramite Pies are revelaed. That's right folks, with profits at the plant tumbling, mean old boss Molluck has come up with the perfect plan for reducing costs and workforce overheads at the same time - and let's just say we're not talking voluntary redundancies here.

Rather unsurprisingly, perhaps, Abe decides that now might be a good time for a change of career and legs it. Companies that measure the performance of their employees in kilograms, however, aren't the sort to respond positively to such action and to get free Abe will have to get past the corporate machine- gun armed robots on the way. There's also the small matter of his fellow Madokan workers at RaptureFarms, who he can't exactly leave to become next week's main course without feeling just a tad guilty, so Abe's mission becomes to get all 40 of his colleagues out of the plant and away, helped only by his distant pal Owen (who communicates with him via the plant's various computer terminals).

Abe is a beautifully animated game, with particular attention given to the movement of its hero in a manner reminiscent of *Prince of Persia*. Abe can walk, run, jump, tiptoe and even roll his way around the processing plant, and you'll need to use all of these movements if you want to achieve your goal. He also can communicate with his fellow workers with a number of simple commands, such as "wait" and "follow me" (luckily, they're very obliging). It's quite a complicated game to control, then, but it's worth sticking with - and you just know it will be as soon as it starts.

Abe would have cost a fortune in the 80s and the hype would probably have been significant too. As it is, it's free and so your duty is to play it and tell others. Go away, go play and go say.

Egghead in Space by Jonathan Cauldwell
(Micro Mart, April 2003)

Egghead in Space is the third in the Egghead series of games by Jonathan Cauldwell, a saga that began some 13 years ago on a CRASH magazine covertape. CRASH - God bless it - is dead now, but Egghead lives on, and in an ironic twist of fate this instalment is the only Egghead title to be commercially released, coming in a time when just about anything Spectrum related has a price of precisely zero pence.

But this is more than just a game. New Spectrum software has been woefully thin on the ground over the last ten years if you don't count the demo scene, and this cuddly little platform frolic might just be the turning point in this sad and sorry state of affairs. Seismic though a new Spectrum title is in its own right, Egghead in Space is actually the first release from nothing less than a brand new software *label* - Cronosoft - and, as I write, a second title, Dead or Alive, has already been released, with a third and a fourth lined up to be deployed very soon to the virtual shop front that is www.cronosoft.co.uk. All of a sudden, our dusty old cups are overflowing, and the man we have to thank for all of this is Simon Ullyatt, the single person the Spectrum community so badly needed to take a chance and invest in some blank cassettes, a ready supply of ink cartridges and a quantity of padded envelopes.

As Spectrum games go, Egghead in Space is as solid as John Prescott's tightly balled fist following his very own egg and head encounter. And every bit as exciting. This is a highly competent piece of 48K coding, smoothly animated with nary a hint of intrusive colour clash to be found. Quite how our oval hero has happened upon eyes, feet and sentience in the first place is a subject unexplored in the accompanying instructions, but what we do know is that mischievous aliens have taken all his Spectrum games and hidden them in an underground labyrinth. Egghead wants them back and it's your job to guide him to them.

It's cheap, it's cheerful and it's fun. And if Cronosoft succeeds in its aim, it's the first of many more titles to come. I urge all Spectrum fans to open their underused wallets and buy this game right now. You won't regret it, and you'll be contributing to something very exciting indeed.

Farmer Jack by Bob Smith/Lee du-Caine
(ZXF, Spring 2007)

Business is not going well for Farmer Jack this year. His wholesome organic homebrew was a big hit in the off-licenses until a nasty competitor came along and flooded the market with cheap plonk. Thankfully the customers weren't fooled by the usual corporate sheen and Jack's sales continued to dominate the market. But the bully-boys aren't going to stop there, it seems... Peering through the curtains one evening, alerted by the fact that clanging, thrashing, mechanical sounds don't ordinarily come from his peaceful fruit allotments, Jack sees metal monsters smashing through his crops, destroying his harvest in front of him.

Each screen in *Farmer Jack in Harvest Havoc* is one of Jack's many allotments. His task is to save his crops from the merciless corporate machinery in one of two ways: he can simply trundle round in his tractor collecting up all his fruit before the monsters get to it, or he can use the supply of boulders scattered around each screen - and a few handy bombs he has - to destroy the monsters. Just be careful to get away from the bombs before the fuse runs out, or tractor parts will be added to the spray of twisted metal left strewn all over the field come morning...

I honestly don't understand the dreadful rating (39%) this game got given by Retro Gamer. Apparently RG editor Darran Jones downgraded the rating from the original figure awarded by the reviewer. Naturally all reviewers have their own preferences and opin-ions vary, but you only have to look at this game - and listen to it - to know instantly that this scores much, much higher than that. Farmer Jack is a simple game, but what it does it does with style. The graphics are extremely pleasing to look at and the music is superb. It's the kind of game your six year old could get into, and to hell with the PSP. In fact, this is exactly the sort of game we need more of to get that generation interested in the Speccy.

Fire and Ice by n-Discovery Group
(YS94, November 2004)

Wizard Druidle is at it again, trying now to melt away Coolmint Island and its peaceful inhabitants. Something's got to be done to stop him, of course - you can't just let whole islands melt away like that - and the person in this case on whose shoulders the problem is to be dropped is novice wizard Dana, especially empowered with Ice Magic by the Queen of the Winter Fairies. Quite why the Queen can't be @##$%&*% to deal with Druidle herself and chooses to delegate such an important job to a newbie isn't made clear, but we can all guess at the sort of quasi-democratic machinery underpinning *those* sorts of decisions. Ahem.

Fire and Ice, by the *n-Discovery Group,* is a simply superb piece of Spectrum software, a brilliantly presented, very addictive puzzle game kind of in the *Boulderdash* ballpark. 89 levels. Excellent music. Great graphics, including some very effective interlacing effects. But there is a catch. *Fire and Ice* is a TR-DOS game, which means it runs from a 640K 3.5" floppy disk connected to your Spectrum via a *Beta Disk Interface* - a British product which didn't sell very well over here, but which was rapidly incorporated into Russian Spectrum clones such as the *Scorpion* and the *Pentagon*. Since it's unlikely you've got any of these lying around, the upshot of it all is that you're going to have to get hold of an emulator supporting TR-DOS if you want to experience this game. It is worth it. You'll be astonished at what it's possible to achieve with a disk system and amazed that we Brits stuck instead with good old cassette tape whilst our Soviet friends laughed themselves sick. Ahhh, the good old days...

Flash Beer by Weird Science Software
(Micro Mart, July 2003)

Is it me, or do Spectrum game characters' wives seem a tad on the tetchy side? First there was Maria, downtrodden Miner Willy's Italian housekeeper (ok - not his wife - but we can't ignore the rumours), of late the star of her very own game - the excellent *Maria vs. Some B£$%ards* - and generally more of a Norah Batty than a Victoria Beckham. But in *Flash Beer*, the latest Boulder Dash clone from Hungarian coders *Weird Science Software*, spouse sadism seems to have reached dizzy new heights.

One can only speculate on the marital mishaps that must have occurred between the Mr and Mrs of this title that such drastic domestic action has come to be taken by this instance of the female of the pixelated species. For, not only has she hidden every last bottle of her husband's favourite brew within the confines of their extremely large house, she has also blocked his way to the bottles with death traps of falling boulders and an uncommonly large number of muscular, merciless guards.

Flash Beer is extremely hard, extremely big and extremely good. For your £2.99 you get not one, not two, but *three* complete games of our hapless hero moving his drunken way from room to room in his search for liquid contentment. If I tell you that game 1 by itself consists of no less than 44 rooms and that I - hopelessly - took ages to get past even the first of these, this should give you some impression of the size and ingenuity of this title. But don't take my word for it: the first game of the trilogy is available as a free download from the WSS website.

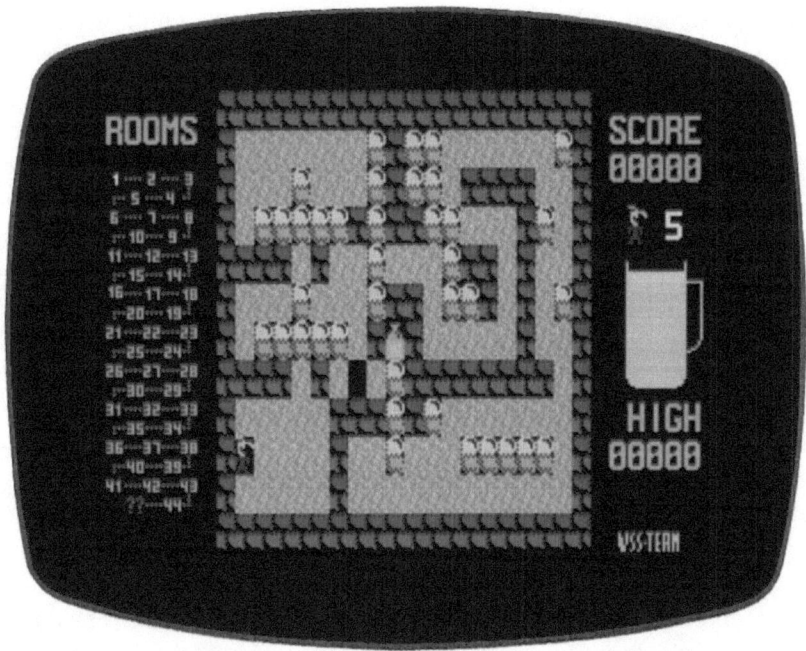

Despite my own shameful performance, I have not been put off by Flash Beer one jot. For one thing, it's an extremely well-presented game that makes clever use of the Spectrum's range of colours. Animation and sound are basic, but for this sort of puzzle game anything more would be obtrusive. What, in fact, you are left with is a great game that just happens to be a Spectrum game, and if you're reading this page out of idle, nostalgic curiosity, I urge you to consider grabbing a (free) emulator (www.spectaculator.com) and downloading this gem just to remind yourself what it's still possible to achieve with 48K, 15 colours and a lot of attention to detail.

It's a puzzle game; it's a Boulder Dash clone. If first person massacres are more your cup of tea then Flash Beer probably won't press any switches for you. But stick with it until you get past the first half of the first screen and then see if you don't want some more. I can think of worse ways of spending no money...

Fun Park by Jonathan Cauldwell
(YS94, November 2004)

We have a lot to thank the *Minigame* competition for. Not only did *TV Game* start out as an entry for the 1k contest, but *Fun Park* was originally the main Spectrum contender for the 2003 4k title. In the end *AmusementPark 4000* - as it was then called - came in second place, but such was its popularity programmer Jonathan Cauldwell promised a 16k version would be developed. And here it is.

Fun Park is Jonathan's fifth title for Cronosoft, sandwiched between shoot-em-ups *Rough Justice* and the forthcoming *More Tea, Vicar?* This one's a strategy game, of course, and the aim is to build an amusement park so big it makes Thorpe Park look like an abandoned slide on a Swindon council estate. Easy it is not. You start the game with a meagre £1,500 and from this point on have to start balancing a budget that includes such outlays as research and development, advertising, security and the funding of a whole range of attractions - from helter-skelters to roller coasters, from cafes and pubs to decorative statues and trees. Bankruptcy is always lurking just around the corner for the first few precarious years of your park's development. You can get a bank loan of an extra £1,000 if you want, but I warn you now the APR is daylight robbery.

Visually, *Fun Park* is a pleasing game to look at, with attractions represented by tidy little icons that flash when a ride is in progress or send little karts, cars or logs whizzing around their tracks and waterways. Visitors are shown as Football Manager style stick people; their animation is about as basic as it gets, yet their antics in the park are bizarrely watchable. Look closely and you'll see some alarmingly loutish behaviour very occasionally, such as the commandeering of a go-kart for a round-the-park joyride - sometimes with tragic consequences (represented by a horizontal stick man). Beefing up security is the only way to deal with this sort of problem, but if you want a laugh, cut right back on the muscle, throw in a couple of pubs next to a log fume and wait. But be warned - fatalities are not good for business.

Rides in the park are accessed via pathways and queuing areas, shown in white and yellow respectively, and it's up to you to organise these properly. The amount of land available to you is not immense and you might find that your initial park layout is a little too generous in its spaciousness later on in the game when

Capitalism With A Social Conscience has outstayed its welcome and you just want to squeeze as much cash from the tourists as you can. Paths, tracks and queuing areas you can redo at will, but attractions can't be pulled down so easily. So Plan ahead.

Fun Park is an immensely addictive game. The detail that's been packed into it (16k, remember) is extraordinary and, for 99p, it's difficult to see how its purchase could be anything other than a truly excellent idea.

Game X by Jonathan Cauldwell
(ZXF, Spring 2007)

Greed is good. Greed is right. Greed, in all of its forms - greed for life, for money, for love, for knowledge, and greed for ZX Spectrum games - has marked the upward surge of humankind. Greed works.

In Jonathan Cauldwell's GameX your mission is to pursue your right to wealth through trading in no less than sixteen titles on the cut-throat Spectrum games market, buying when their value is low, selling when their value is high (please note, share prices can go down as well as up). In addition to the money you make through games that perform well, you can also accrue capital by playing games you've bought shares in (your score is converted directly to capital).

The games range from *Muncher*, a Pac-Man clone and the first of the games you encounter (you play this as soon as you start to raise some initial investment capital), to *Skatepig*, a Manic Miner style platformer with a pig on a skateboard (naturally); from *Rescue*, a Thrust style gravity basher, to *Mr. Spud*, a burger construction task also seen as a minigame in Cauldwell's recent *Egghead 4 - Egghead Entertains*. And so on. Of course, it's not all fun and sound effects: death in GameX comes in the form of the taxman (a clever pairing of life's two certainties), who catches up with you just as soon as your tax score (incremented each time you have an encounter with a nasty in any of the games) reaches 100%.

In case you're wondering, 16 into 48 goes just three times (that's right, GameX is not a multiload), so that's 3K per game that Cauldwell's had to play with here - and that's before you take into account such factors as screen memory (that's 6K gone, for starters), the actual trading element of the game (share prices are displayed down the right hand side of the screen), the intro screen, the high score table and a whole host of other memory eaters. Cauldwell's well known for his ability to cram more into a byte than a supersized Mcburger, but here he's just getting cheeky.

One has to wonder what goes on in the mind of Jonathan Cauldwell that a pig on a skate-board should suggest itself as a natural variant of the Manic Miner theme. Pigs and pork pro-ducts do seem to crop up a great deal in his games, how-ever, and who am I to interfere with any therapeutic process he should choose to work such issues through? Personal development issues aside, GameX is sheer quality, which you realise from the moment you see the superb loading screen. How all these games - *each with their own levels* - have been squeezed into 48K is beyond me; each title would be a worthy 16K game in its own right. My one piece of advice would be to avoid buying into 'The Dead' - because that's the social group to which you will belong if you try to play it.

Higgledy Piggledy by Jonathan Cauldwell
(ZXF, Summer 2005)

Another year; another *Cronosoft* release; another game by Jonathan Cauldwell. The first that the denziens of WoS Forums knew of this upcoming release was Cronosoft's Simon Ullyatt asking for entries in an inlay designing competition. A very strange thread followed, but Simon got his entries nonetheless and the cover for Higgledy Piggledy is one of the best Cronosoft inlays so far.

The game? It's to do with Interplanetary Pig Farmer Eadwig Addlethorpe. Of course it is. Eadwig's pigs - through some sort of odd evolutionary quirk - can fly; this, of course, is not normal porcine behaviour and frankly it makes things rather awkward for Eadwig when it comes to rounding them up for slaughter. He's installed a number of teleporters - like you do - in order to send them off to the pig processing plant, but can he direct those pigs successfully into the teleporter? He cannot. And that, of course, is where you come in.

If it was down to me a rifle and a pointer dog would do the trick quite nicely; instead we are given a fiendishly addictive puzzle game where you both move around the playing area and attempt to influence the direction of the pigs by picking up and moving blocks one at a time. The pigs, you see, move along in straight lines until they hit a block, at which point they take a right-angled turn. It's a bit like a combination of Lemmings and that game where you control the light with the mirrors. But more frustrating. Oh yes - and better.

In my opinion Jonathan Cauldwell has already made a permanent name for himself in Spectrum software, simply due to the fact that it's the twenty-first century and he's the only guy around banging out Spectrum games at the frequency and high quality that he is. All of his games to date have been highly competent, attractive and fun-to-play pieces of work but, with the possible exception of Fun Park, I can't say in all honesty that anything he's done so far stands out as a Specrum classic in its own right. But Higgledy Piggledy does.

There are a number of simple, but very effective ways in which he achieves this - we're not talking multicolour effects or border graphics here, just striking visuals and simple gameplay. The backgrounds against which Eadwig and pigs move in particular are cleverly managed patchworks which look like they shouldn't be possible on a Spectrum. Of course you quickly realise that the effect has more to do with good colour placement than it does any tomfoolery with the TV beam, but by then the illusion has done its work and what you're left with is a 'look' that will now always be associated with this specific game. Higgledy Piggledy has that ultra-special quality: it doesn't look like something you've seen before. Add in a wacky series of title screen animations (pigs flying; sausages sizzling: you know the sort of thing) and you have something completely unique. I've applauded Jonathan's work before, but this gets an ovation.

Iron Sphere by Ian Munro
(ZXF, Spring 2007)

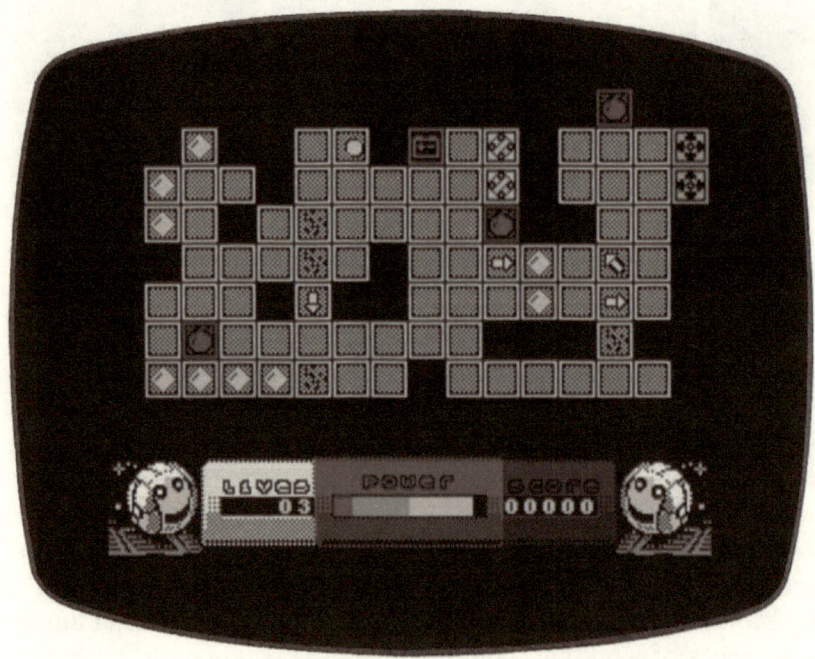

By now, mad professors really should have learned to be more wary of thunder storms. As men of science, the usefulness of a good lightning conductor where the protection of top secret laboratories and their illegal experimentation is concerned should have been disseminated long ago. Alas, the inhibition of short-term gratification for the sake of long-term benefit just doesn't seem to interest the likes of Prof. Roland Iron-Sphere. Like many others before him, his laboratory's been hit by a stray lightning bolt and he now finds himself transported into his own experiment. He's only himself to blame.

In fact, Professor Iron-Sphere is now an actual iron sphere. Who would have thought a random discharge of electricity could have such a sense of irony? In order to escape from this nightmare, Rolly - as he's known to his friends - must now collect up at least one diamond from each of the screens he passes through. Once he starts rolling, by the way, he can't stop, so if you end up falling into the inky darkness below or colliding with a bomb it's because you didn't plan ahead enough. There are all sorts of tricks on each screen to make this more complicated still, such as platforms that crumble once you've passed over them and arrows that throw you in their direction (whether it's safe to do so or not).

Izzy Wizzy by Jonathan Cauldwell
(ZXF, Spring 2007)

Those pesky Commodore fundamentalist mutants. You thought our hero Izzy saw them off with his weapons-grade confectionary in *Gloop*, didn't you? Well, they're back. And this time they've plans so evil I hesitate even to speak of them.

We've all spared a thought or two every now and then to those *"what would have happened if the Loki had been built?"* sort of discussions; now consider for a moment a chilling alternative: *What would have happened if the Spectrum had never been built?* 25 years on from the pivotal moment in history that was April 1982, that's exactly what the CFMs intend to find out. Those dastardly fellows have somehow managed to get their hands on the plans for a time machine; once built, they intend to use it to prevent the Sinclair ZX Spectrum from ever being invented. Yes.

As luck would have it, Izzy is on the case once more. In the years since his last encounter with these decidedly unsavoury characters he's learned that bubble gum isn't always the most efficient method for dealing with today's brand of well-equipped bad guy and obtained himself instead a bronze certificate in magic. That's right. The spells he can now cast include 'hover' (freeze a mutant in mid-air), 'mutate' (turns mutants into, er, other mutants) 'diddums' - as in 'ahh' (increase your energy by one point), 'turnaroo' and 'speedy' (slow mutants down). Be careful, though: not all spells work on all mutants. And it's not like Izzy can just cast them straightaway, either - for each spell he first has to collect all the ingredients required for it, and even then spells can't be cast until he's also acquired plenty of 'magic points' with which to cast them. By sheer chance, however, those clumsy CFMs have left all the ingredients you need just lying around in their secret hideaway castle whilst they work on their time machine (as we all know, baddies' Achilles' Heel is to leave lying around the place all the bits and pieces required to bring about their demise) and magic points can be accrued by picking up the playing cards also lying around in the castle (and maximised further by gambling on them).

Your magic and magic points are only there to help you along your way, however; the key to your ultimate success lies in good, old fashioned explosives. Three of the CFMs' bombs have been left - you guessed it - lying around the castle for you to find. They have in this case at least had the good sense to encrypt the bombs' arming mechanisms, however, so to arm them you have to crack a 4 digit code sequence. Despite the fact that this is a code put together by Commodore enthusiasts and therefore not likely to tax you too much, this job stresses you mightily and your energy drains whilst you do it. So be quick.

At first, Izzy Wizzy (by Jonathan Cauldwell) looks like a fairly standard platformer - the sort of thing that could perhaps be put together with something like Platform Games Designer with a little bit of love. But then you start noticing and getting into all the extra bits, like the little games of *Play Your Cards Right* and the bomb code cracking sequence - stuff that you can't help think doesn't need to be there and yet it's a particularly nice touch that it is. Working out which spells you have and which will work on any particular screen is tricky, but it's this sort of detail that draws you into the game and keeps you involved in it once the initial novelty has worn off.

And when it's all over and the dust has settled, don't shed any tears for those CFMs. They were going to use those bombs at 25 Willis Road, you know. Just you think about that, son; just you think about that.

Justin by CNGSOFT/Radastan
(ZXF, Spring 2007)

Justin's finally hit the motherload... or has he? Slipping silently across the moonlit lawn, the mansion appears to ooze money. Unfortunately for Justin, the owner's discovered the benefits of exotic plants and creatures as an effective security system. Poisonous plants and creatures, that is...

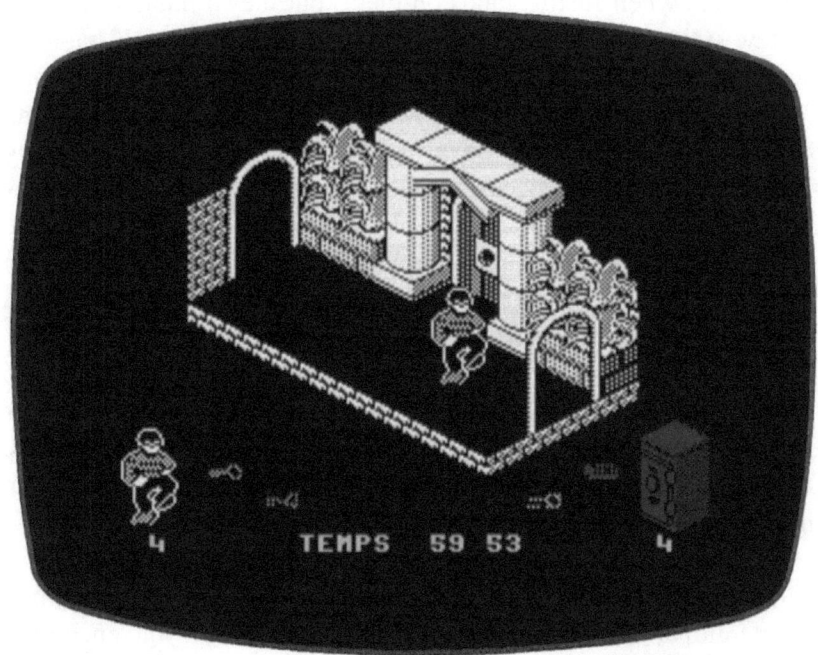

Justin is a tribute to 1988 Spanish Dinamic release *Dustin* (which was also translated and released in the UK as a YS covertape, although at the 'Play again?' prompt the translators forgot that the English for *si* is *yes* and you had to press 'S' to continue...) and other unspecified titles. It's a beautifully presented 3D isometric game (and we haven't seen any of those for a while) in which your mission is to locate and blast open the four safes of the mansion and feast on the gold within. Justin was originally written for the Amstrad CPC and this is a Spectrum port, with graphics by Radastan.

Inside the mansion, Justin must avoid the venomous imports and patrolling guards, and solve a variety of puzzles left for him in order to get around the mansion and locate door keys, the safes and the TNT he needs to crack them open. And he has just one hour to do it in. As he moves furtively around the mansion, the clock at the bottom of the screen ticks away...

To find the various bits and pieces he needs, Justin often finds himself having to use the blocks he encounters in rooms to serve his purpose. Some blocks can be moved by pushing them, some disintegrate when Justin stands on them (but they'll hang around for the few split seconds necessary for you to launch yourself back off them towards the next one, so they do have some use). In one room, a guard walks round in circles carrying a block on his head and that's pretty much all you have to work with. Getting the timing right on your jumps is occasionally very, very important; Justin has the rather handy skill of being able to change direction whilst he flies through the air mid-jump (that's the criminal mind, you see - no respect for the laws of motion). You will need to use this skill on a number of screens if you're going to progress to the next one.

With all those meanies floating around whilst you're trying to achieve pixel-perfect precision jumping, you could be forgiven for finding Justin just a tad on the hard side. Luckily a cheat exists, (thanks to 'goodboy' at WoS for pointing it out): enter GOODY at the define keys menu and you get infinite lives.

First the criticisms: Justin is a hard game, made harder in places by occasional incidences of what are either bugs in the programming or intentional cheating bastness. The first spider you encounter moves straight through the plant in the middle of the room, for example, and there's a green room with a raised platform around deadly plants where, inexplicably, you fall between the first two squares. If goodboy hadn't posted his infinite lives cheat on WoS, I think I would have ended up screaming at this game. The drawing of Justin seems a little at odds with the isometric perspective and I miss the tick-tock footsteps of the Ultimate classics.

But never mind any of that; this is a great game that matches the scope of any of the 3D games of the eighties. The graphics are an absolute treat and there are plenty of puzzles between those screens where a pixel in the wrong direction means death. So there you have it: ZX Spectrum isometric games still being written in the 21st century; talk about fantastic.

Manic Miner: Neighbours by Andrew Broad
(ZXF, Christmas 2004)

Ok. I admit it. I'm beginning to worry about Dr Andrew Broad. The obsession with Manic Miner and Jet Set Willy I could assimilate. The integration of Smithsonian and Tolkensian themes in Manic Miner: The Hobbit / Jet Set Willy: The Lord of the Rings I could manage. I could handle the fact that my life would have to be completely dedicated to the works of Broad if ever I was actually going to complete a single level of one of his games. But this release takes things just one step too far.

Manic Miner: Neighbours - Allana Truman, the latest of Andrew's MM/JSW titles, is dedicated to sci-fi geek Allana Truman, Andrew's favourite Neighbours character of all time. In the game you play Allana's Boyfriend Lance Wilkinson and - just as it was in the 'real thing' - you have to perform seven labours in order to win Allana as your girlfriend and then sort a few extra head-scratchers in order to say ta-ta to Aussieland and hot foot it the pair of you up to America. Yes.

As with all Broad MM/JSW games, MM:N-AT is difficult to a degree that makes you want to squeeze lemon juice in your eyes. This time round we do have an 'easy version,' however (you might complete it before you reach retirement age), and an infy lives poke in the README file. All I can say is bring back Madge Bishop.

Maria verses some bastards by Ericx1
(ZXF, Summer 2003)

If I'm brutally honest, *Manic Miner* and its numerous sequels never really did all that much for me. I appreciate the significance of the game and - don't get me wrong - I don't *dis*like the game, but beyond filling a few dull moments of boredom or work avoidance it services no major need for me. One aspect of my indifference to the genre - probably the major one - is the graphics. To me they're pretty much of a muchness, samey, nothing to write home about. And so on. Yes, I'm aware I've missed the whole point, but there just isn't enough there to get me to it.

Which is why Maria vs some bastards took me so completely by surprise. The graphics are, quite simply, superb. Without using any special machine code tricks; simply by using Spectrum colour intelligently, Erix1 - author of this, one of the latest MM games to be released via the extremely industrious Manic Miner and Jet Set Willy Yahoo! Group - has created one of the most visually stunning Spectrum titles I have ever seen. Many of the screens, in fact, look as though they could easily have stepped right off an 8-bit console, that's how good they are. I've always thought that BRIGHT was seriously underused in Spectrum colour and looking at this game I now feel completely justified in that view. I can't help but feel that if this game had appeared mid 80s the Spectrum world would have gone nuts about it.

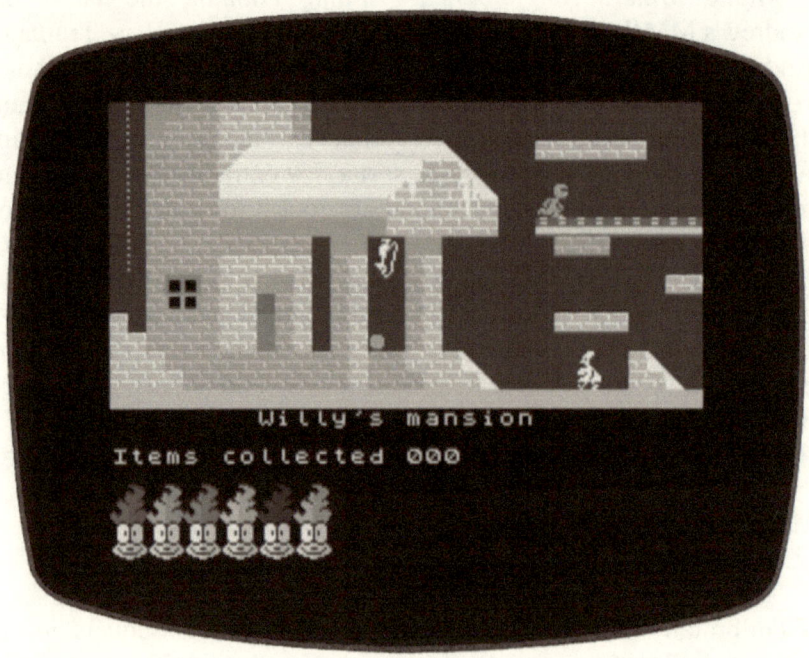

Oh yes, the plot. Well it's this: Miner Willy has gone and got himself kidnapped by some very naughty ninjas and is being held for ransom (do ninjas really do the ransom thing?) for the pricey sum of 240 items. So Maria, Willy's long-suffering and much misunderstood housekeeper (she's a softy at heart really) is off to fetch these for him. It's kind of a spin-off really - or one of those sequels where they can't afford to get the original actors involved.

I'm really into this game, and MM/JSW fans will no doubt be pleased to know I am now spending time thinking about the puzzles. Now I want to see the next screen, see? And then the one after it. And the one after that. And maybe I might get converted to the genre along the way.

Platform Games Designer by Jonathan Cauldwell
(ZXF, Christmas 2004)

Honestly, it's ridiculous. I can't remember being so excited about a new Spectrum release as I have been about Platform Games Designer since... well, I just can't remember a time. Perhaps the release of PAW is the nearest benchmark. In one sense it really doesn't matter to me whether PGD turns out to be any good or not because I've enjoyed the anticipation so much.

But now the wait is over and it's time to be judgemental. Well I'm going to give my verdict straight away: I *love* Platform Games Designer and I can see an alarmingly large portion of the Christmas break being spent on it. It's one of the most addictive pieces of Spectrum software I've seen in a very long time.

And I'm starting with that statement because I do have improvement suggestions to make and I want everyone to be clear that these don't distract me from thinking PGD is just fabulous. But more on them later.

First of all, there are actually two versions of PGD - I'm not clear at the moment whether these are to be sold as one package or separately. The *Linear Designer* allows you to create games where you must collect a number of objects in a room in order to be able to pass onto the next level. Think Manic Miner. The *Explorer Designer*, on the other hand, allows you to wander around, from room to room as you damn well please. Think Jet Set Willy. If you're a MM/JSW fan that will no doubt please you a great deal. If, on the other hand, you frequently find yourself wandering what on earth all the fuss is about this genre of game, you might find your spirits deflating ever so slightly at this piece of information. In fact, the similarities between the MM/JSW games and the parameters of PGD are many. You create objects to collect and magic doors that open on their acquisition. You create 'patrolling nasties' that move around on pre-deter-mined paths and kill you instantly with their touch. And you can create crumbling platforms and conveyor belts. All ala MM/JSW.

But of course you don't actually have to create any of these if you don't want to (well, ok, the doors you kind of do need). And therein lies the key. Stop thinking about MM/JSW and start thinking about what you can actually do with these tools and you'll soon find the software allows an immense variety of environments.

For starters, the graphical possibilities are quite considerable. You are given an endless number of 'blocks' - basically 8x8 character cells - from which to build your rooms; you design these in pretty much the same way that you would design UDGs except that you also choose the block's properties (solid block, platform, conveyor, object, etc). Then in the screen layout area you simply select the blocks you want and drop them in place. It's as simple as that.

For the main 'hero' sprite you get 16x16 pixels to play with and 8 frames of animation - that's actually 16 frames in total because the hero uses a different sprite for walking left as s/he does for walking right. The patrolling nasties also occupy 16x16 pixels but only get four frames of animation. I'm guessing that you could use a patrolling nasty as an animated 4 character block if you were to restrict its patrol route to a static location (eg, for a crackling fire), but I must confess I couldn't for the life of me manage to get the patrolling nasties screen working (perhaps because I imported a game designed on an earlier version of PGD).

Which brings us to the wish list. This divides nicely into two groups - features which I would really like to be added and features which would be just nice if added. Both lots, of course, would be likely to take a considerable chunk out of the memory available to your game if implemented. Do we actually mind about that? I have to say I wouldn't mind at all - I'd rather put together a more 'deluxe' game that had fewer levels than a very large game without the bells and whistles. But that's just me.

Features which I would really like to be added. Sound effects. There are none. You can put together a tune in the music editor, which is nice, of course, but I would far rather have no music and spot sound effects. Obviously this is easier said than done, since making a sound effects editor would probably not be very 'cost effective' in terms of the memory required to create it. A compromise would be to create a 'bank' of pre-coded effects. PGD could hold, say, 10 of these at a time, which you could assign to specific events (jump, walk, pick up objects, etc), whilst additional 'banks' of effects could be held on cassette and loaded separately. *Slopes.* It would be really nice to be able to walk up and down slopes. As it is surfaces are either horizontal or vertical. *Pass behind objects.* It would be great if you could define blocks as 'pass behind' to give the illusion of depth - for example pillars the sprite moves behind or walls with windows in them (like Dan Dare). *Thrust.* I'm thinking JetPac here - or Bombjack. A sort of 'superjump' where vertical movement continues as long as the jump key is pressed. Something like that.

Features which would be just nice. Drop. Although it might appear at first that there can't be all that much use for a 'drop object' function in a platform game, it did become an issue when I was designing my little Father Christmas game. Think about it... *Shoot!* A gun would be great. But I imagine it would be quite hard to include, since you would then need to define the graphics for both the bullets/laser beams and the explosions for all the various sprites and blocks. *Block browser.* Once you've created a few blocks, looking through them one at a time can be a little difficult to get your head around. All that white space at the bottom of the screen could be put to good use by using it to display a scrolling line of all of your blocks to select from. I reckon.

So PGD is superb, but it could be even better still. And if there is ever a version two I think I'll find myself getting all excited in anticipation yet again. In the meantime I think PGD could be significant enough anyway to initiate a whole new era within the Spectrum community. Something like an 'Annual PGD compo' sounds in order. What do you think?

Rough Justice by Jonathan Cauldwell
(Micro Mart, February 2004)

Once again a Spectrum release from Cronosoft, and once again it's by Jonathan Cauldwell, the embodiment of the 80s bedroom programmer updated for the 21st Century. And *Rough Justice* is something special in its own right: this is a brand new title *written for* the new Spectrum market (although I ask you to interpret that term loosely please), rather than a previously unreleased game dusted down and given a new polish.

There's an element of cinematic tension built into Rough Justice, with its white-text-on-black-background intro reminiscent of the trailer to a big budget blockbuster; all that's missing is the gravely voice and a punchy, one line catchphrase: *Justice is about to be served,* or something of that ilk. But in fact, the drama began with this particular title before even the first quantity of £2.99 changed hands for its shiny, cassette-encased being. Until the last minute, Rough Justice was shrouded in secrecy, and that last minute was its unveiling at the Norwich ORSAM show last November. Early versions even shipped with a bug that crashed the program at the end of every game. Put that in your pipe and smoke it Microsoft.

The plot? Rough Justice sees aggrieved niece Shipley - pilot's license fresh in her hands - taking on the nasty aliens that have kidnapped her uncle, intergalactic bounty hunter (and cyborg to boot) Mansfield Rough. The game is a screen-by-screen, no-going-back shoot 'em up in the style of Cybernoid genre; a mayhem of missiles, aliens and crates to shoot at with your lasers (you also have an inexhaustible supply of bouncing bombs, which is rather handy) as you work your way through the many, many levels.

Rough Justice is a slick enough game if you play it on a 48K Spectrum: Cauldwell's sprites bounce around the screen with their trademark smoothness, colour is used well with no hint of attribute clash, and you could ask no more from your ship in terms of its responsiveness. Load it into a Spectrum 128, however, and the game starts to rock. The soundtrack by Polish AY enthusiast Yerzmyey adds a whole new dimension; let me tell you, an evening with Rough Justice loaded into Spectaculator on my PC, with the volume turned up all the way, was the most fun I've had in ages. Yerz, incidentally, is the organizer of the *AY Riders*, a multinational group of musicians dedicated to squeezing every last drop of creativity out of the Spectrum 128's AY chip (you can download their 3 free MP3 albums at *http://ayriders.zxdemo.org/*), so the quality of this music should come as no surprise.

The collaboration doesn't end there either. Across the waters, Tommy Pereira has once again put his artistic talents to use in a simply superb loading screen that uses just about every trick there is to pack colour and detail in together. And Tommy is also responsible for the game's inlay card.

I haven't got through to the end of Rough Justice yet; quite simply, I don't know if I'll live long enough, the game is so big. I will point out that the furthest I've managed so far was a cavern on level 3 or 4 which wouldn't let me exit – possibly a bug, but I was playing with an infinite lives cheat at the time, so I can't say I feel hard done by. The one gripe I do have is with the little "+1"s that appear when you blast certain crates. Plus one *what?* Precisely nothing appears to increment by one when you acquire them!

An enormous game at a considerably less than enormous price; Rough Justice is another landmark in Cronosoft's journey. If you're not bothered by the physical presence of an actual cassette, by the way, you can now purchase emulator tape files from their website at a reduced price. Head over to *www.cronosoft.co.uk* to find out more.

Turbomania by Jonathan Cauldwell
(ZXF, Spring 2007)

It's not easy being six times Formula Retro racing champion, Tim Wrangle. One minute you're basking in a lifestyle of burning rubber, chequered flags and spurting champagne; the next a freak hole in the fabric of space and time transports you from a carefree practice lap to a sinister parallel universe where Formula Retro is a different sport altogether. One that bears more than a passing resemblance to Pac-man, in fact...

Turbomania was a Cauldwell release in late 2005 for the 16K Spectrum. Your task is to drive your Formula Retro car over every inch of the track - turning it blue in the process - whilst avoiding the evil baddie cars out to get you. Along the way various treats pop up to increase your score or fuel, or to freeze the baddies still for a few seconds. Oh yes, and there's a traffic camera too - that's not a treat at all, oh no...

Of course, Cauldwell being Cauldwell, it can't be just that on its own. Clearly determined to make every last byte of that 16K work for him, there's a whole host of other bits and pieces thrown in, making Turbo-mania feel a very complete title for a 16K game. At the press of a key you can reconfigure the maze, for example, so that bits previously boxed in become accessible (and you might just box in one of your your pursuers too). There are also quite a number of little games you can play to get an extra life at the end; these include a symbol matching game, a traffic light reaction speed test (hit the right colour when it displays), a quick car race in the fashion of Decathalon (watch that keyboard now) and a Simon-esque 'follow the leader' memory game. Shoe-horn, anyone?

16K, you say? 16K?? Aren't 16K games supposed to consist of three screens with a dragon at the end? How did all this fit into 16k? Ok, I suppose the mini-games by themselves can't take up all that much room; the thing is, each time you encounter a new one you're left wondering just how much there is in Turbomania you've yet to see. This is top notch stuff. Now wouldn't it be great if someone somehow could squirt it into a ROM cartridge?

TV Game by Weird Science Software
(YS94, November 2004)

Is it the future or is it the past? Players unfamiliar with the Spectrum's limitations might consider *TV Game* to be a definite rewind down the video-game timeline. It is, after all, a version of Pong - a game hardly known for its bells and whistles.

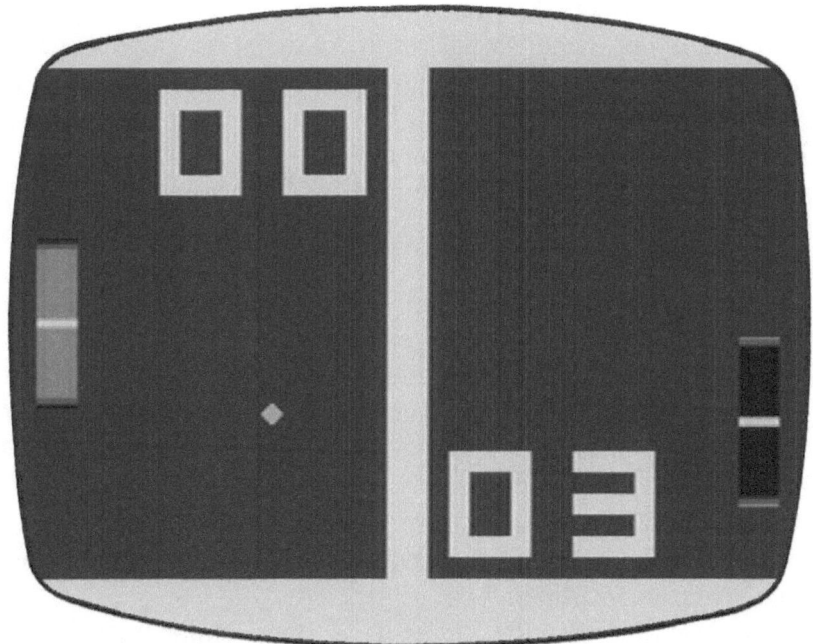

Look more closely, however, whilst at least pretending to know a thing or two about our rubber-keyed friend (stroke your chin and nod thoughtfully whilst looking), and you might notice that this particular implementation of Pong is actually rather cheeky. In fact, it shows blatant disregard for The Rules - The Rules being 1) you can't do anything in the Spectrum border other than change its colour and 2) you can't display more than two colours per 8x8 character.

Before hard-core Speccy sceners set upon me with rolled-up copies of *The Complete Spectrum ROM Disassembly* I should point out that rules (1) and (2) aren't actually true at all if you're a

Proper Machine Code Programmer. Plenty of games have given a one-fingered salute to the two colour rule in their high-score tables and a few have even strayed into the Border Zone from time to time (anybody remember the handlebars in *Paperboy*?). But these border effects were very rarely a part of the actual game play and they were nearly always static. Whereas *TV Game's* multicolour bats move up and down in the border quite merrily in response to your key presses, as though to do so is a quite trivial matter that no-one ever thought of before.

TV Game's programmer has assured me that creating this game was anything but trivial. *Papp Gyorgy* became a Spectrum fan in 1983 when he saw *Harrier Attack* on his grandparents' machine. He made a number of subsequent attempts to learn machine code, but only really got to grips with it in 2000 when his speccy club decided to start writing new software. *TV Game* - originally intended as an entry into the 1k *Minigame* online competition - was where he really honed his skills. And those bats in the border caused him some major headaches.

He discovered, for example, that issue 2 and issue 3 Spectrums (Sinclair released several versions of the original 48k motherboard) behave slightly differently in their interrupt timings, producing significantly different results in the all-important border area. Hence the calibration screen you get once the game's loaded up, through which the game determines what issue Spectrum it's running on.

I said earlier that *TV Game* is a Pong clone; actually its inspiration was those plug-it-into-your-telly bat-and-ball games that appeared in Pong's wake. Boasting several games-in-one, all were actually identical, except the playing area was red for tennis, green for football and white for hockey. The bat size changed too. Needless to say, this sort of genius was best appreciated with a) mates and b) several pints of lager. So it is too with *TV Game,* the implementation of which is basically flawless. There's no sound - impossible with all the border stuff going on, but a beep or two would have jollied things along nicely. Apart from this it does exactly what's promised on the tin.

So it's the future *and* the past - mixed up and sprinkled generously with irony. Which makes it a 21st-Century title in every respect. I recommend it wholeheartedly.

Appendix C
'Depth' program listing

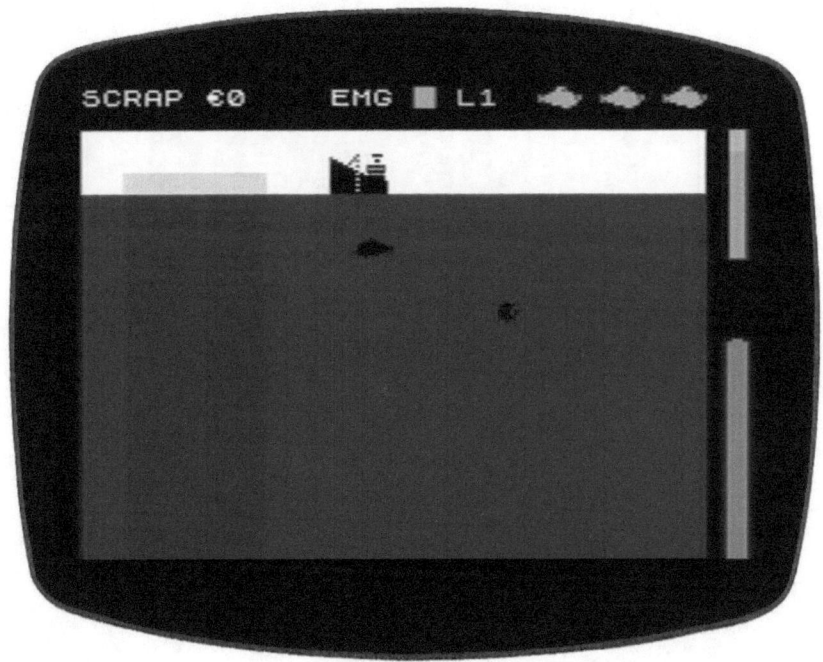

It is the year 2206. The seas have risen. The soil has gone. Humankind now salvages what it can from the ocean floor. In *Depth*, you must guide your minisub down into the dark depths of the ocean to seek out scrap metal. The deeper you go, the darker it gets. Luckily, your sub's powerful light can penetrate the inky darkness for a short distance. Keep an eye on your battery, though; too much use of the light will soon run it flat. As you get close to objects beneath you, your electromagnet display will flash green to let you know a useable object is below and red/yellow when the EMG is active and an object attached. There are also mines to avoid, which your EMG sensor can detect, but only weakly.

To guide your sub, use keys Q for up, A for down, O for left and P for right. Space bar turns the sub light on and off.

Program

```
   10 PAPER 0: INK 0: BORDER 0: CLS
   20 POKE 23658,8
   30 GO SUB 8000
   40 LET x=13: LET y=7: LET ox=15: LET oy=11: LET d=0: LET od=0: LET v=0: LET ov=0: LET l=0: LET depth=1: LET ytop=5: LET sbtop=6: LET dtr=0: LET vtr=0: LET sub=2: LET level=3: LET score=0
   50 LET battery=2000: LET bcounter=10: LET bcycle=25: LET bplot=79: LET carry=0: LET final=0
   60 DIM g(3,16): RESTORE 8500: FOR m=1 TO 3: FOR n=1 TO 16: READ a: LET g(m,n)=a: NEXT n: NEXT m
   70 DIM i(3): LET i(1)=4: LET i(2)=3: LET i(3)=4
   90 GO SUB 5500
  500 LET dead=0
  505 BRIGHT 1: PAPER 0: INK 7: PRINT AT 0,0;"SCRAP U";score;AT 0,12;"EMG": BRIGHT 0: PAPER 5: INK 0: FLASH 1: PRINT AT 0,15;" ": INK 5: PAPER 0: PRINT AT 0,16;" ": FLASH 0
  510 GO SUB 5100
  900 REM screen loop
  920 BRIGHT 1: PAPER 5: INK 1: PRINT OVER 1;AT depth+1,31;" ": IF depth>1 THEN BRIGHT 0: PRINT OVER 1;AT depth,31;" "
  925 IF depth<6 THEN BRIGHT 0: PRINT OVER 1;AT depth+2,31;" "
  930 GO SUB 6500: BRIGHT wbr
  935 FOR n=2 TO 21
  940 IF n<ytop THEN PAPER 7: PRINT AT n,0;"
  945 IF n>=ytop THEN PAPER wpa: PRINT AT n,0;"
  950 NEXT n
  955 IF level=1 AND depth=1 THEN BRIGHT 0: PAPER 7: PRINT AT 4,2;"
  960 IF level=2 AND depth=1 THEN BRIGHT 0: PAPER 7: PRINT AT 4,1;"
  965 IF level=3 AND depth=1 THEN BRIGHT 0: PAPER 7: PRINT AT 4,4;"
 1010 DIM s(22,30): LET final=0
 1015 IF level=1 AND depth=1 THEN RESTORE 8125: GO SUB 4000
 1020 IF level=1 AND depth=2 THEN RESTORE 8130: GO SUB 4000
 1025 IF level=1 AND depth=3 THEN RESTORE 8135: GO SUB 4000
 1030 IF level=1 AND depth=4 THEN RESTORE 8140: GO SUB 4000
 1035 IF level=1 AND depth=5 THEN RESTORE 8145: GO SUB 4000
```

```
1040 IF level=1 AND depth=6 THEN
   RESTORE 8150: GO SUB 4000
1045 IF level=2 AND depth=1 THEN
   RESTORE 8165: GO SUB 4000
1050 IF level=2 AND depth=2 THEN
   RESTORE 8170: GO SUB 4000
1055 IF level=2 AND depth=3 THEN
   RESTORE 8175: GO SUB 4000
1060 IF level=2 AND depth=4 THEN
   RESTORE 8180: GO SUB 4000
1065 IF level=2 AND depth=5 THEN
   RESTORE 8185: GO SUB 4000
1070 IF level=2 AND depth=6 THEN
   RESTORE 8190: GO SUB 4000
1075 IF level=3 AND depth=1 THEN
   RESTORE 8205: GO SUB 4000
1080 IF level=3 AND depth=2 THEN
   RESTORE 8210: GO SUB 4000
1085 IF level=3 AND depth=3 THEN
   RESTORE 8215: GO SUB 4000
1090 IF level=3 AND depth=4 THEN
   RESTORE 8220: GO SUB 4000
1095 IF level=3 AND depth=5 THEN
   RESTORE 8225: GO SUB 4000
1100 IF level=3 AND depth=6 THEN
   RESTORE 8230: GO SUB 4000: LET
 final=1
1490 IF depth=1 THEN BRIGHT 1: P
APER 7: PRINT AT 3,12;"HIJ": PRI
NT AT 4,12;"■FG": PAPER 1: PLOT
106,134: PLOT 106,132
1500 GO SUB 2500
1600 IF utr=1 THEN LET depth=dep
th-1
1605 IF dtr=1 THEN LET depth=dep
th+1
1620 IF depth>1 THEN LET ytop=2:
 LET sbtop=3
1630 IF depth=1 THEN LET ytop=5:
 LET sbtop=6
1640 IF dtr=1 THEN LET y=ytop+1
1650 IF utr=1 THEN LET y=20
1670 LET utr=0: LET dtr=0: LET o
y=y
1900 IF dead=0 THEN GO TO 900
1905 IF dead=1 AND sub<>-1 THEN
GO TO 500
1910 IF dead=1 AND sub=-1 THEN G
O TO 40
2490 STOP
2500 REM movement
2510 BRIGHT wbr: PAPER wpa
2520 IF d=0 THEN PRINT AT y,x;"A
B": IF carry>0 THEN GO SUB 4700
2522 IF d=0 THEN GO SUB 5000: IF
 l=1 THEN GO SUB 6200: GO SUB 60
00
2530 IF d=1 THEN PRINT AT y,x;"C
D": IF carry>0 THEN GO SUB 4700
2532 IF d=1 THEN GO SUB 5000: IF
 l=1 THEN GO SUB 6250: GO SUB 61
00
2540 LET oy=y: LET ox=x: LET od=
d: LET ov=v: LET v=0
2545 IF depth=1 AND X=13 AND Y=6
 THEN GO SUB 4200
2550 IF l=1 THEN LET battery=bat
tery-1: LET bcycle=bcycle-1: IF
bcycle=1 THEN GO SUB 5300
```

```
2555 IF carry>1 THEN LET battery
 =battery-1: LET bcycle=bcycle-1:
 IF bcycle=1 THEN GO SUB 5300
2560 LET bcounter=bcounter-1: IF
 bcounter=0 THEN LET battery=bat
tery-1: LET bcycle=bcycle-1: LET
 bcounter=10
2565 IF s(y+1,x)>1 OR s(y+1,x+1)
>1 THEN BRIGHT 1: PAPER 4: INK 0
: FLASH 1: PRINT AT 0,15;" ": IN
K 4: PAPER 0: PRINT AT 0,16;" ":
 FLASH 0: INK 0
2567 IF s(y+1,x)<3 AND carry=0 T
HEN BRIGHT 0: PAPER 5: INK 0: FL
ASH 1: PRINT AT 0,15;" ": INK 5:
 PAPER 0: PRINT AT 0,16;" ": FLA
SH 0: INK 0
2570 IF bcycle=1 THEN GO SUB 530
0
2575 IF carry>0 THEN GO SUB 3010
: GO TO 2680
2580 IF IN 57342=189 AND x>0 THE
N IF s(y,x-1)=2 THEN GO SUB 4500
: LET dead=1: GO TO 2999: REM le
ft mine
2590 IF IN 57342=190 AND x<28 TH
EN IF s(y,x+2)=2 THEN GO SUB 450
0: LET dead=1: GO TO 2999: REM r
ight mine
2600 IF IN 57342=189 AND x>0 AND
 s(y,x-1)<1 THEN LET x=x-1: LET
d=0: GO TO 2500: REM left
2610 IF IN 57342=190 AND x<28 AN
D s(y,x+2)<1 THEN LET x=x+1: LET
 d=1: GO TO 2500: REM right
2620 IF IN 64510=190 AND y>sbtop
 THEN IF s(y-1,x)=2 OR s(y-1,x+1
)=2 THEN GO SUB 4500: LET dead=1
: GO TO 2999: REM up mine
2630 IF IN 64510=190 AND y>sbtop
 THEN IF s(y-1,x)<1 AND s(y-1,x+
1)<1 THEN LET y=y-1: LET v=2: GO
 TO 2500: REM up
2640 IF IN 64510=190 AND y=sbtop
 AND depth>1 AND final=0 THEN LE
T utr=1: GO TO 2999: REM up scre
en
2645 IF IN 64510=190 AND y=sbtop
 AND final=1 THEN IF d=1 AND x=2
8 THEN LET utr=1: GO TO 2999: RE
M up from final screen
2650 IF IN 65022=190 AND y<21 TH
EN IF s(y+1,x)=2 OR s(y+1,x+1)=2
 THEN GO SUB 4500: LET dead=1: G
O TO 2999: REM down mine
2660 IF IN 65022=190 AND y<21 TH
EN IF s(y+1,x)<1 AND s(y+1,x+1)<
1 THEN LET y=y+1: LET v=1: GO TO
 2500: REM down
2665 IF IN 65022=190 AND y<21 TH
EN IF s(y+1,x)>2 AND s(y+1,x-1)<
3 THEN LET carry=s(y+1,x): BRIGH
T 1: INK 2: PAPER 6: FLASH 1: PR
INT AT 0,15;" ": INK 6: PAPER 2:
 PRINT AT 0,16;" ": FLASH 0: BRI
GHT 0: INK 0: GO SUB 4400: GO TO
 2500: REM get cargo
2670 IF IN 65022=190 AND y=21 AN
D depth<6 THEN LET dtr=1: GO TO
```

```
2999: REM down scoreeen
2680 IF dead=1 THEN GO TO 2999
2682 IF dtr=1 THEN GO TO 2999
2684 IF utr=1 THEN GO TO 2999
2688 IF IN 32766=190 AND l=1 THE
N LET l=0: GO SUB 6700: GO TO 25
00: REM light on
2690 IF IN 32766=190 AND l=0 THE
N LET l=1: GO TO 2500: REM light
 off
2700 GO TO 2550
2999 RETURN
3000 REM movement + cargo
3010 IF IN 57342=189 AND x>0 THE
N IF s(y,x-1)=2 OR s(y+1,x-1)=2
THEN GO SUB 4500: LET dead=1: RE
TURN : REM left mine
3020 IF IN 57342=190 AND x<28 TH
EN IF s(y,x+2)=2 OR s(y+1,x+2)=2
 THEN GO SUB 4500: LET dead=1: R
ETURN : REM right mine
3030 IF IN 57342=189 AND x>0 AND
 s(y,x-1)<1 AND s(y+1,x-1)<1 THE
N LET x=x-1: LET d=0: GO TO 2500
: REM left
3040 IF IN 57342=190 AND x<28 AN
D s(y,x+2)<1 AND s(y+1,x+2)<1 TH
EN LET x=x+1: LET d=1: GO TO 250
0: REM right
3050 IF IN 64510=190 AND y>sbtop
 THEN IF s(y-1,x)=2 OR s(y-1,x+1
)=2 THEN GO SUB 4500: LET dead=1
: RETURN : REM up mine
3060 IF IN 64510=190 AND y>sbtop
 THEN IF s(y-1,x)<1 AND s(y-1,x+
1)<1 THEN LET y=y-1: LET v=2: GO
 TO 2500: REM up
3070 IF IN 64510=190 AND y=sbtop
 AND depth>1 AND final=0 THEN LE
T utr=1: RETURN : REM up screen
3075 IF IN 64510=190 AND y=sbtop
 AND final=1 THEN IF d=1 AND x=2
8 THEN LET utr=1: RETURN : REM u
p screen
3080 IF IN 65022=190 AND y<20 TH
EN IF s(y+2,x)=2 OR s(y+2,x+1)=2
 THEN GO SUB 4500: LET dead=1: R
ETURN : REM down mine
3090 IF IN 65022=190 AND y<21 TH
EN IF s(y+2,x)<1 AND s(y+2,x+1)<
1 THEN LET y=y+1: LET v=1: GO TO
 2500: REM down
3100 IF IN 65022=190 AND y=21 AN
D depth<6 THEN LET dtr=1: RETURN
 : REM down screen
3500 RETURN
4000 REM screen array
4005 INK 0
4100 READ a
4110 IF a=1 THEN READ b: READ c:
 READ e: FOR n=b TO 21: FOR m=c
TO (c+e-1): LET s(n,m)=1: PAPER
bpa: BRIGHT 0: PRINT AT n,m;" ":
 NEXT m: NEXT n
4115 PAPER wpa: BRIGHT wbr
4120 IF a=2 THEN READ b: READ c:
 LET s(b,c)=2: PRINT AT b,c;"E"
4125 IF a=9 THEN GO TO 4140
4130 GO TO 4100
```

```
4140 FOR n=1 TO 16 STEP 4: IF g(
level,n)=depth THEN LET ly=g(lev
el,n+2): LET lx=g(level,n+3): LE
T lv=g(level,n+1): LET s(ly,lx)=
lv: LET s(ly,lx+1)=lv: PRINT AT
ly,lx;CHR$ (154+((lv-3)*2)): PRI
NT AT ly,lx+1;CHR$ (155+((lv-3)*
2))
4150 NEXT n
4190 RETURN
4200 REM recharge & unload
4205 FOR i=12 TO 21: BRIGHT 1: P
APER 3: INK 0: PRINT AT i,31;" "
: NEXT i: BEEP 0.05,50: LET batt
ery=2000: LET bplot=79
4207 IF carry>0 THEN LET score=s
core+(carry*25)
4210 IF carry>0 THEN LET carry=0
: PAPER wpa: BRIGHT wbr: INK 0:
PRINT AT y+1,x;"  "
4215 BRIGHT 1: PAPER 0: INK 7: P
RINT AT 0,7;score: BRIGHT 0: PAP
ER 5: INK 0: FLASH 1: PRINT AT 0
,15;" ": INK 5: PAPER 0: PRINT A
T 0,16;" ": FLASH 0: INK 0
4220 RETURN
4400 REM REMOVE CARGO FROM SCREE
N & ARRAY
4410 LET s(y+1,x)=0: LET s(y+1,x
+1)=0
4420 FOR n=1 TO 16 STEP 4
4430 IF g(level,n)=depth THEN IF
 g(level,n+2)=y+1 AND g(level,n+
3)=x THEN FOR r=0 TO 3: LET g(le
vel,n+r)=0: NEXT r
4440 NEXT n
4490 RETURN
4500 REM bang!
4505 PAPER 6: CLS : PAPER 7: CLS
 : PAPER 0: CLS
4510 FOR n=60 TO 50 STEP -1: BEE
P 0.05,n: NEXT n
4520 PAUSE 100: INK 7: PRINT AT
9,7;"SUB ";ABS (sub-3);" LOST TO
 MINE": PAUSE 100: IF sub>1 THEN
 PRINT AT 14,9;"Press enter...":
 PAUSE 0
4525 IF sub=0 THEN PRINT AT 14,1
1;"Game over": PAUSE 100
4530 LET sub=sub-1: LET depth=1:
 LET battery=2000: LET bplot=79:
 LET carry=0: LET l=0: LET x=13:
 LET y=7
4550 RETURN
4700 REM draw carried objects
4710 IF y<21 THEN PRINT AT y+1,x
;CHR$ (154+((carry-3)*2)): PRINT
 AT y+1,x+1;CHR$ (155+((carry-3)
*2))
4800 RETURN
5000 REM clear sub
5010 IF OY>Y AND carry=0 THEN PR
INT AT y+1,x;"  "
5012 IF OY>Y AND carry>0 AND y<2
1 THEN PRINT AT y+2,x;"  "
5014 IF OY<Y THEN PRINT AT y-1,x
;"  "
5020 IF OX<X THEN PRINT AT oy,ox
;"  ": IF carry>0 AND y<21 THEN P
```

```
RINT AT oy+1,ox;" "
5030 IF OX>X THEN PRINT AT oy,ox
+1;" ": IF carry>0 AND y<21 THEN
 PRINT AT oy+1,ox+1;" "
5040 RETURN
5100 REM Instruments
5110 BRIGHT 0: INK 1: PAPER 5: P
LOT 248,159: DRAW 0,-48: DRAW 7,
0: DRAW 0,48
5120 FOR i=2 TO 7
5155 PAPER 5: PRINT OVER 1;AT i,
31;" "
5170 NEXT i
5180 FOR i=12 TO 21: PAPER 3: IN
K 0: PRINT AT i,31;" ": NEXT i
5190 PAPER 0: BRIGHT 1: INK 3: P
LOT 248,80: DRAW 7,0: PLOT 250,8
1: DRAW 3,0
5200 FOR i=28 TO 28-(sub*3) STEP
 -3: BRIGHT 0: INK 5: PRINT AT 0
,i;"CD": NEXT i
5290 RETURN
5300 REM battery indicator
5305 INK 0: BRIGHT 1: PAPER 3: P
LOT 249,bplot: DRAW 5,0: LET bpl
ot=bplot-1: LET bcycle=25
5320 RETURN
5500 REM START SCREEN
5505 FOR N=1 TO 30: BEEP 0.005,N
: NEXT N
5510 PAPER 7: INK 0: BORDER 0: B
RIGHT 1: CLS
5520 PRINT AT 1,13;"DEPTH": PLOT
 104,159: DRAW 39,0
5525 FOR N=3 TO 21: PAPER 1: PRI
NT AT N,0;"
        ": NEXT N
5530 INK 7: PRINT AT 4,6;"It is
the year 2206";AT 6,6;"The seas
have risen": PRINT AT 7,7;"The s
oil has gone"
5535 PRINT AT 8,1;"Humankind now
 salvages what it";AT 9,4;"can f
rom the ocean floor"
5540 PRINT AT 11,2;"Guide your m
inisub down into";AT 12,2;"the d
arkness; seek out scrap"
5545 PRINT AT 13,4;"with your el
ectro-magnet": INK 5
5547 BRIGHT 0: FOR N=15 TO 21: P
APER 1: PRINT AT N,0;"
         ": NEXT N
5550 PRINT AT 16,4;"        Q:up
A:Down"
5555 PRINT AT 17,4;"        O:left
P:right"
5560 PRINT AT 18,4;"SPACE turns
light on/off"
5570 FOR N=20 TO 21: PAPER 0: IN
K 7: PRINT AT N,0;"
         ": NEXT N
5575 PRINT AT 21,0;"Written by C
olin Woodcock, using"
5580 POKE 23659,0
5585 PRINT AT 22,0;"BASin Releas
e 12b, compiled with"
5590 PRINT AT 22,31'"The HiSoft
BASIC compiler v. 1.1"
5595 POKE 23659,2
```

```
5600 PAUSE 0
5610 INK 7: PAPER 0: CLS
5900 RETURN
6000 REM left light matrix - vert
6005 IF y=oy THEN GO SUB 6300: GO TO 6080
6010 FOR c=3 TO 2 STEP -1
6020 FOR r=1 TO 5
6030 IF c=2 AND r>1 AND r<5 THEN GO SUB 6600: GO TO 6060
6040 IF c=3 AND r=3 THEN GO SUB 6600: GO TO 6060
6050 GO SUB 6650
6060 NEXT r
6070 NEXT c
6080 RETURN
6100 REM right light matrix - vert
6105 IF y=oy THEN GO SUB 6400: GO TO 6180
6110 FOR c=6 TO 7
6120 FOR r=1 TO 5
6130 IF c=7 AND r>1 AND r<5 THEN GO SUB 6600: GO TO 6160
6140 IF c=6 AND r=3 THEN GO SUB 6600: GO TO 6160
6150 GO SUB 6650
6160 NEXT r
6170 NEXT c
6180 RETURN
6200 REM Face l; erase r
6205 IF d=od THEN GO TO 6240
6210 FOR c=7 TO 8
6215 FOR r=2 TO 4
6220 GO SUB 6650
6230 NEXT r
6235 NEXT c
6240 RETURN
6250 REM Face r; erase l
6255 IF d=od THEN GO TO 6290
6260 FOR c=2 TO 1 STEP -1
6265 FOR r=2 TO 4
6270 GO SUB 6650
6280 NEXT r
6285 NEXT c
6290 RETURN
6300 REM left light matrix - hor
6310 FOR c=3 TO 2 STEP -1
6320 FOR r=2 TO 4
6330 IF c=2 THEN GO SUB 6600: GO TO 6360
6340 IF c=3 AND r=3 THEN GO SUB 6600: GO TO 6360
6350 GO SUB 6650
6360 NEXT r
6370 NEXT c
6380 RETURN
6400 REM right light matrix - hor
6410 FOR c=6 TO 7
6420 FOR r=2 TO 4
6430 IF c=7 THEN GO SUB 6600: GO TO 6460
6440 IF c=6 AND r=3 THEN GO SUB 6600: GO TO 6460
6450 GO SUB 6650
6460 NEXT r
6470 NEXT c
```

```
6480 RETURN
6500 REM colours
6510 IF depth=1 THEN LET wbr=1:
LET wpa=1: LET bpa=1
6520 IF depth=2 OR depth=3 THEN
 LET wbr=0: LET wpa=1: LET bpa=0
6530 IF depth>3 THEN LET wbr=0:
 LET wpa=7: LET bpa=0
6540 RETURN
6600 REM light cell
6610 IF (y-(3-r))>21 OR (x-(4-c)
+1))>30 THEN GO TO 6630
6615 IF s(y-(3-r),x-(4-c))=1 THE
N BRIGHT 0: PAPER 7: PRINT OVER
1;AT (y-(3-r)),(x-(4-c));" ": GO
 TO 6630
6620 BRIGHT 1: PAPER 5: PRINT OV
ER 1;AT (y-(3-r)),(x-(4-c));" "
6630 RETURN
6650 REM dark cell
6660 IF (y-(3-r))>21 OR (y-(3-r)
)<ytop THEN GO TO 6680
6663 IF (x-(4-c)+1)>30 THEN GO T
O 6680
6665 IF s(y-(3-r),x-(4-c))=1 THE
N BRIGHT 0: PAPER bpa: PRINT OVE
R 1;AT (y-(3-r)),(x-(4-c));" ":
GO TO 6680
6670 BRIGHT wbr: PAPER wpa: PRIN
T OVER 1;AT (y-(3-r)),(x-(4-c));
" "
6680 RETURN
6700 REM light off
6710 IF d=0 THEN GO SUB 6750
6720 IF d=1 THEN GO SUB 6800
6730 RETURN
6750 FOR c=3 TO 2 STEP -1
6760 FOR r=2 TO 4
6770 GO SUB 6650
6780 NEXT r
6790 NEXT c
6795 RETURN
6800 FOR c=6 TO 7
6810 FOR r=2 TO 4
6820 GO SUB 6650
6830 NEXT r
6840 NEXT c
6845 RETURN
8000 REM udgs
8010 FOR A=USR "A" TO USR "U"+7
8020 READ user: POKE A,user
8030 NEXT A
8040 RETURN
8050 DATA 3,5,31,191,191,127,63,
14,128,192,240,253,255,253,224,0
,1,3,15,191,255,191,7,0,192,160,
248,253,253,254,252,112
8060 DATA 153,126,118,251,251,12
6,126,153,217,255,223,255,223,25
5,223,255,80,248,248,252,252,252
,252,252,0,0,128,224,249,254,255
,255
8070 DATA 0,32,64,160,0,35,130,2
27,0,240,0,96,0,248,168,248,15,1
7,39,75,19,99,255,127,240,1,255,
254,192,192,128,0
8080 DATA 124,73,73,127,255,255,
249,112,0,0,0,192,192,224,224,19
2,31,63,127,255,255,127,63,31,24
```

```
0,241,247,255,255,247,241,240
8090 DATA 3,5,9,63,127,127,55,8,
192,32,32,224,224,240,96,128,255
,146,146,255,255,255,255,18,254,
74,74,254,254,255,254,72
8100 DATA 0,28,34,120,120,34,28,
0
8110 REM screen data
8115 REM level 1
8125 DATA 1,5,2,7,2,10,20,9
8130 DATA 1,2,2,7,1,15,15,4,1,8,
24,4,2,10,13,9
8135 DATA 1,2,2,7,1,1,15,4,1,1,2
4,4,2,5,12,9
8140 DATA 1,2,2,7,1,1,15,4,1,1,2
4,4,2,8,13,2,15,22,9
8145 DATA 1,2,2,7,1,1,15,4,1,1,2
4,4,2,8,13,2,15,22,9
8150 DATA 1,2,2,7,1,1,15,4,1,17,
20,3,1,1,24,4,2,15,22,9
8160 REM level 2
8165 DATA 1,5,1,8,9
8170 DATA 1,2,1,8,1,8,15,1,2,10,
13,2,13,11,2,10,23,9
8175 DATA 1,2,1,8,1,1,15,1,1,8,1
4,3,2,13,11,9
8180 DATA 1,2,1,8,1,1,14,3,1,6,1
2,7,2,4,11,2,7,9,9
8185 DATA 1,2,1,8,1,1,12,7,1,15,
20,2,1,10,23,5,2,10,9,2,11,20,2,
7,26,9
8190 DATA 1,2,1,8,1,1,12,7,1,1,2
0,2,1,1,23,5,2,7,11,2,4,9,2,21,2
8,9
8200 REM level 3
8205 DATA 1,5,4,5,9
8210 DATA 1,2,4,5,1,5,12,5,1,8,2
3,5,9
8215 DATA 1,2,4,5,1,2,12,5,1,2,2
3,5,9
8220 DATA 1,2,4,5,1,2,12,5,1,2,2
3,5,9
8225 DATA 1,2,4,5,1,2,12,5,1,2,2
3,5,1,21,4,24,9
8230 DATA 1,2,1,1,1,5,26,3,2,5,3
,2,5,4,2,5,5,2,5,6,2,5,7,2,5,8
8235 DATA 2,6,7,2,7,6,2,8,5,2,9,
4
8240 DATA 2,10,3,2,10,4,2,10,5,2
,10,6,2,10,7,2,10,8
8245 DATA 2,5,11,2,6,12,2,7,13,2
,8,14,2,9,15,2,10,16
8250 DATA 2,10,11,2,9,12,2,8,13,
2,7,14,2,6,15,2,5,16
8255 DATA 2,5,19,2,5,20,2,5,21,2
,5,22,2,5,23,2,5,24
8260 DATA 2,6,19,2,7,19,2,8,19,2
,9,19,2,10,19
8265 DATA 2,7,20,2,7,21,2,7,22,2
,7,23,9
8490 REM cargo data
8500 DATA 2,5,14,16,6,6,21,11,6,
4,21,13,6,3,16,20
8510 DATA 4,3,5,12,6,4,21,10,5,3
,14,20,0,0,0,0
8520 DATA 6,7,21,3,6,7,21,5,6,7,
21,7,6,7,21,9
```

Index

128Ke, 93

25 Willis Road, 133, 156
256 colour overlays, 85

3-8910/12 Emulator (AY utility), 58

AGD (Arcade Games Designer), 54
AIR file format, 45
Akton Films, 140
Albo, Julián, 52
AlchNews disk magazine, 39
Alone Coder, 91
Alphacom 32 printer, 32
Altwasser, Richard, 84
Amstrad CPC64, 128
Amstrad Plc, 4, 5, 15, 17, 93, 135, 137, 158
AMX mouse, 35, 89, 109
Android emulators, 89, 91, 104, 108, 109, 110
assembler, 48, 52, 53, 90
audio/video recording, vii, 46
AY chip/music, 36, 37, 58, 59, 78, 89, 165
AY Riders, 58, 165
AYFX Editor, 59
Ayo, Iñigo, 85

Barker, Andy, 64
Barnett, Tony, 64

BASIC, 2, 6, 7, 22, 36, 39, 52, 53, 54, 55, 56, 62, 65, 66, 67, 68, 69, 70, 71, 72, 73, 74, 75, 82, 84, 90, 91, 98, 106, 108, 131, 132, 138
compiling, 53, 54, 66, 69, 70, 71, 74
BASIC loader, 6, 7, 12, 71, 72, 73, 74, 75
BASin, 52, 53, 54, 55, 66, 67, 68, 69, 70, 72, 138
Bebbington, Shaun, xi, 27, 129
beeper, 41, 58, 59
BeepFX sound utility, 59
BETA disk interface, 6, 78, 80, 81, 88, 148
BMP2SCR, 52
border effects, 28, 167
Bradbeer, Robin, 132, 138
Broad, Andrew, 159
Brown, Steve, 64, 142
Bulba, Sergey, 58

C5 electric vehicle, 134, 141
Carroll, Martyn, xi
Cascade Cassette 50, 49, 65, 66
cassette files, vii, 5, 7, 8, 9, 10, 11, 12, 34, 40, 42, 58, 72, 75, 79, 90, 99, 137, 165
creating new cassettes, 9, 10, 63
Cauldwell, Jonathan, 26, 54, 98, 106, 112, 145, 150, 151, 152, 153, 155, 156, 161, 163
Chandler, Richard, 91

Cheetah SpecDrum, 36
Cheveron, 98
Chocano, Javier, 86, 87
CNGSOFT, 157
Codemasters, 24, 27
colour effects, 28
Commercial Breaks documentary, 139
comp.sys.sinclair, 26, 49, 136, 142
converting cassettes to TZX format, 64
Cowley, Chris, 91
Crap Games Competition, 49, 65
CRASH magazine, 131, 134, 136, 141, 145
Cronosoft, 26, 55, 65, 137, 145, 146, 150, 152, 163, 165
Currah
  µsource, 90
  µSpeech, 36, 37
Curry, Chris, 140

Dalby, Tom, 106
Datel, 36, 38, 40
deathsoft, 91
debugger, 69, 87, 90, 91, 93, 109
demo scene, 27, 28, 79, 145
Demotopia website, 28
Dickinson, Rick, 128, 133
Didaktik Gama, 89
disk files, 13, 19, 39, 79, 81, 82, 92
DivIDE hard disk interface, 37, 87, 90, 94, 95, 96, 97
Dorigatti, Alessandro, 98
Dorling Kindersley, 138
DSK file format, 13, 18, 19, 62
du-Caine, Lee, 146
Dunn, Paul, xi, 2, 52, 55, 56
Durell, 107

EightyOne emulator, viii, 42, 43, 80, 84, 85, 90, 95
Elite Collection, ix, 107
Elite Systems, 107
EmuZWin, viii, 85, 99

Ericx1, 159
Es.pectrum, viii, 86, 87
Expandor SoftROM, 37

Fayzullin, Marat, 89, 109
Foreman, Dave, 142
Format magazine, 38, 95, 135
Format Magazine, 38
FORTH, 84
Fry, Dan, 63
Fuller AY Box, 36, 37
Fuse emulator, viii, 87, 89, 95, 102, 110, 137

G+DOS, 41
G+DOS (Plus D Operating System, 39
Gamebase ZX database utility, 60
Garabik, Radovan, 137
Gee, S. M., 138
Gibart, Jocelyn, 63
Gomez, Jamie Tejedor, 50
Gordon, Bruce, 136
Gosh Wonderful ROM, 22, 23
Goti, David, 85
Grachev, Denis, 106
Granada Publishing, 138
Grant, John, 132
Gremlin Graphics, 107
Grimwood, Jim, 141
Gyorgy, Papp, 167

Hayne, Cameron, 70, 71
HDF file format, 95, 96
heat sink, 4
Hewson, 107
HiSoft, 54, 66, 69, 70, 71
Humphries, Nick, xi, 44, 46, 139, 141

Imagine Ltd, 27, 133, 139
INDUG (Disciple/Plus D User Group), 38
Infocom, 19
input recording, 44, 45, 46
Investronica, 77, 86, 134

iOS emulators, 55, 105, 107

Jahn, Claus, 51, 61, 63, 72, 75
James, Mike, 138
Jolly, Derek, 52
Jones, Darran, 137, 147
joystick, 21, 29, 30, 31, 35, 44,
  107, 108, 109, 113, 133
  Kempston interface, 30, 31
  Quickshot, 29, 30
  Sinclair, 30
Jupiter Ace, 84
Juric, Zeljko, 91, 92

Kac, Tomaz, 137
Kapartzianis, Vaggelis, 93
Kendall, Philip, 23, 87
keyboard, vii, 3, 4, 18, 21, 22, 30,
  78, 97, 108, 109, 110, 111, 113,
  127, 130
Kladov, Vladimir, 85
KLP2, 98

La Puerta de Sinclair (film), 140
Lambda 8300, 84
Lancaster, Garry, 88
Lancaster, Gary, 97
LCD, 52
Lens Key utility, 85, 86
Lenslok, 85
Little Shop of Pixels, 106
loading screen, 6, 7, 12, 72, 73,
  75, 152, 165
loading tones, 2, 6, 8, 9, 10, 41,
  42, 97
Logan, Ian, 139
López-Grao, Juan Pablo, 64
Lunter, Gerton, 1, 47, 93

machine code, 6, 48, 53, 54, 69,
  71, 72, 73, 74, 75, 132, 138
Magnetic Scrolls, 19, 20
Magnum Lightgun, 36, 37
MakeTZX utility, 63, 64, 65
Making the most of the Micro TV
  series, 139

manuals, 15, 25, 53, 56, 57, 68,
  70, 71, 132, 138
Marvin emulator, ix, 108, 109
MB02 hard disk interface, 95
McKay, James, 92
MDR file format, 13, 16, 17
Melbourne House, 48, 138, 139
Melodik AY-3-8912 Soundbox,
  36, 37
MGT, vii, 6, 12, 37, 39, 79, 87, 88,
  92, 109, 135, 136
MGT Disciple disk interface, 37,
  38, 39, 79, 88, 89, 92, 109, 135
MGT Plus D disk interface, vii, xi,
  6, 12, 36, 37, 38, 39, 40, 41, 79,
  88, 135
MIA (Missing In Action), 24, 64,
  65
Micro Mart, xi, xiii, xiv, 27, 127,
  129, 143, 145, 148, 163
Micro Men BBC film, 140
Miles, Alan, 136
Minigame competition, 27, 106,
  150, 167
Muhi, Miklos, 91
Multiface, 33, 35, 36, 38
Munro, Ian, 154

Nair, Arjun, 92
n-Discovery Group, 147
Needle, Jonathan, xi, 2, 12, 105
Nikki, 98
Nine Tiles Software, 132
Nintendo DS emulator, 104, 110

O'Hara, Frank, 139
Ocean, 131, 139
Opus Discovery disk system, 87,
  88
Outlet disk magazine, 39
Owen, Andrew, xi, 22, 23, 90, 98
Owen, Chris, 141
Owen, Simon, 85

Palace, 107
Palette Editor utility, 98, 99

Pasmo, 52
Pentagon, 1, 78, 79, 80, 81, 87, 89, 90, 109, 110, 112, 135, 148
Pereira, Tommy, 165
PGD (Platform Games Designer), 55, 156, 161
Piggot, Colin, 130
Planet Sinclair website, 141
Plíva, Pavel, 50
POKE, 44
Prestel Micronet, 101
Prism VTX5000 Modem, 101
PZX file format, 112

Radastan, 157, 158
Rak, Patrik, 110
Ramsoft, 63, 64, 88
Raspberry Pi, 56
RealSpectrum emulator, viii, 45, 88, 95
Realtime, 106
Retro Gamer magazine, xiii, 27, 137, 139, 141, 147
Ribic, Samir, 91, 92
Richard, 84, 91, 108
Ringo R470, 84
Rodin, Dmitry, 110
Rodriguez, Jose, 53
Rollings, Andrew, 139
ROM cartridges, 20, 21, 30, 133
Romantic Robot, 35, 36, 38
RS232 serial port, 15, 16, 31, 32, 34, 35, 41
RWAP Software, 94
RZX file format, xv, 45, 46, 87, 112

SAM Computers, 136
Sam Coupé, 130
SAM Coupé, 135, 136
SCL file format, 79, 80
Scorpion, 1, 79, 81, 87, 89, 109, 110, 136, 148
SCR file format, 48, 50, 52
screenshot saving, 47
SE BASIC, 23

SE Basic ROM, 22
SEUD (Shoot 'Em Up Designer), 55
SevenuP, 50, 51, 53
SGD (Spectrum Games Database), 24, 60
Shiru, 59
Sinclair flat-screen pocket TV, 133
Sinclair Programs magazine, 133
Sinclair QL, 15, 26, 84, 130, 134
Sinclair Research Ltd, 2, 5, 13, 133, 134
Sinclair User magazine, 133, 136, 142
Sinclair, Clive, 131, 133, 135, 139, 140
Sintech, 94
Smith, Bob, 146
Smith, Chris, 97, 139
SMT, 91
SNA file format, 12, 13
snapshot files, vii, xv, 11, 12, 16, 39, 45, 58, 85, 108, 112
Spec256 emulator, 85, 99
SpecBAS, 55, 56, 57
Speccy emulator, viii, ix, 28, 41, 45, 61, 89, 101, 109, 110, 130, 147, 166
Speccy Search Bar, 61
Spectaculator emulator, ix, 1, 2, 4, 7, 8, 9, 12, 13, 16, 18, 19, 22, 23, 28, 31, 33, 34, 35, 39, 40, 41, 42, 44, 45, 46, 47, 48, 52, 55, 60, 63, 70, 71, 73, 79, 80, 82, 83, 90, 93, 105, 106, 107, 109, 137, 165
Spectranet, 87, 102
Spectrum +2, 4, 84, 129, 135, 138
Spectrum +2A, 4, 135
Spectrum +3, 1, 4, 5, 13, 17, 18, 19, 20, 38, 90, 135
    disk system, 4, 5, 12, 13, 17, 18, 79
Spectrum +3e, 87, 88, 97, 110

Spectrum 128, 1, 4, 9, 10, 13, 16, 17, 21, 38, 39, 41, 58, 77, 81, 84, 86, 91, 108, 134, 135, 143
Spectrum 16K, 2, 17, 26, 37, 56, 84, 91, 97, 132, 133, 152
Spectrum 48K, xiv, 1, 2, 3, 5, 9, 10, 16, 17, 22, 27, 36, 84, 91, 108, 127, 128, 133, 134, 149, 152
Spectrum screen display, 50
Spectrum Tape Loader, 63
Spectrum Tape Preservation Project, 65
Spectrum+, 3, 4, 13, 134, 138
Spud emulator, viii, 91, 98
Sugar, Alan, 4, 128
Sweeney, Gerard, 44, 61, 142
SZX file format, 12, 13, 112

Tang, William, 48, 138
TAP file format, 7, 9, 13, 52, 54, 58, 63
Tape Explorer utility, 63
tape hiss/wobble, 10, 42, 91
Tape utilities, viii, 63
Taper utility, 63
Tasword, 32, 34, 35, 41
TC2048, 78, 84, 89, 90, 91, 109
TC2068, 78
Television display, vii, 41
Thompson, Paul, 60
Thompson, Tony, 51
Thumb Candy documentary, 140
Timex, 32, 77, 78, 80, 84, 86, 87, 89, 90, 91, 109, 110
Tipshop website, 44, 60, 107, 112, 142
TK85, 84
toast rack, 4
Tommy Gun, 51
Total Computer Gang, 143
Tracker AY software, 58
TRD file format, 62, 79, 80, 92
TR-DOS, xi, 78, 79, 80, 81, 82, 87, 92, 148
TS1000, 77, 84

TS1500, 77, 84
TS2068, 77, 78, 80, 84, 89, 109
TZX file format, xv, 7, 9, 13, 27, 62, 63, 64, 65, 72, 75, 112, 137, 142
TZX Vault website, 39, 142

UDGs (User Defined Graphics), 53, 68
ULA chip, 90, 97, 98, 133, 139
ULAplus, xi, 87, 90, 91, 93, 98, 99, 100, 113
Ullyatt, Simon, 65, 145, 152
Ultimate, 24, 158
UnrealSpeccy emulator, viii, 91
USR 0 mode, 143

van der Heide, Martijn, xi, 24, 60, 63, 64
vbSpec, viii, 91
Vehmaa, Sami, 87, 88, 89, 97
Vickers, Steven, 84, 132, 138
vitamin_caig, 58
Vortex Tracker AY utility, 58

Warajevo emulator, viii, 91, 92, 93, 136
Wearmouth, Geoff, 22
Weird Science Software, 28, 148, 167
West Coast Computers, 136
Westcott, Matthew, xi, 28
Wilson, Matthew, 141
Winston, 102
WinZ80 emulator, 93
Woodmass, Mark, 90, 96
World of Spectrum website, xi, xiii, xv, 2, 19, 24, 25, 26, 27, 28, 40, 48, 52, 58, 59, 60, 61, 63, 64, 65, 79, 83, 87, 88, 90, 91, 92, 93, 98, 101, 102, 106, 108, 109, 110, 112, 137, 138, 139, 141, 142, 152, 158
Wynne, Mike, 42, 43, 80, 84

X128, viii, 92

YASPIC (Yet another Spectrum Image Convertor), 52
Yerzmyey, 165
Your Sinclair magazine, xi, xiii, 27, 46, 132, 135, 136, 137, 139, 141, 143
Your Sinclair Rock 'n' Roll Years documentary, 46, 139, 141
website, 141
Your Spectrum magazine, 96, 134, 135, 141

Z80, 84
Z80 emulator, viii, 1, 47, 93, 136
Z80 file format, 12, 13
Z88, 135
Zenobi Software, 39, 106
Zero emulator, viii, 92, 93
ZX BASIC Compiler, 53, 54
ZX Interface 1, 13, 14, 15, 16, 17, 20, 37, 39, 87, 89, 90, 133
ZX Interface 2, 20, 21, 30, 87, 133
ZX Maps Creator, 50
ZX Microdrive, 1, 5, 13, 14, 15, 16, 17, 39, 133
ZX Net, 37
ZX Printer, 1, 31, 32, 33, 34, 47, 89, 90, 91, 109
ZX Screens, 50, 52
ZX Spectrum SE, 84, 87, 98, 110
ZX SPIN, 2, 8, 9, 10, 11, 13, 16, 18, 19, 22, 23, 31, 33, 36, 37, 39, 40, 42, 44, 46, 47, 48, 52, 53, 55, 63, 79, 80, 81, 82, 83, 90, 93, 95, 98, 99, 100
ZX Tunes website, 58
ZX32 emulator, viii, 93
ZX80, 84, 97, 131, 132
ZX81, 26, 31, 32, 77, 78, 84, 85, 97, 127, 128, 132, 133
ZX97 Lite, 84
ZX-Assembler utility, 62
ZXATASP interface, 87
ZX-Blockeditor utility, 62, 63, 75, 76
ZX-Central utility, 61
ZXCF interface, 87, 88, 89, 97
ZXdroid emulator, ix, 110
ZXDS emulator, ix, 110, 111, 112, 113
ZX-Editor utility, 62
ZX-Explorer utility, 61
ZXF magazine, xiii, xiv, 1, 27, 127, 129, 143, 146, 151, 152, 154, 155, 157, 159, 161
ZX-Favourites utility, 62
ZX-Gamestatistics utility, 62
ZX-Modules, 52, 61
ZX-Paintbrush, 52, 62, 72, 73
ZX-Preview utility, 62
ZXtune AY utility, 58
ZZ Spectrum emulator, 25, 60

www.ingramcontent.com/pod-product-compliance
Lightning Source LLC
Chambersburg PA
CBHW030936180526
45163CB00002B/588